Prefabulous

Prefabulous

The house of your dreams, delivered fresh from the factory

SHERI KOONES

The Taunton Press

The Taunton Press
Inspiration for hands-on living®

The Taunton Press, Inc., 63 South Main Street, PO Box 5506, Newtown, CT 06470-5506

e-mail: tp@taunton.com

Editor: Bridget Biscotti Bradley

Jacket/Cover design: Alison Wilkes

Interior design: Alison Wilkes

Layout: Cathy Cassidy

Illustrator: Chuck Lockhart

Cover Photographers: Front cover (top) Courtesy Vetter Windows and Doors; (bottom left) courtesy Innsbrook Custom Homes; (bottom right) Courtesy Engerman Contracting; Back cover (top) Photo by Roger Wade; (bottom) Photo by Art Grice; Author photo by Studio A.

Library of Congress Cataloging-in-Publication Data

Kooncs, Shcri, 1949-

 Prefabulous : the house of your dreams, delivered fresh from the factory / Sheri Koones.

     p. cm.

 Includes bibliographical references and index.

 ISBN-13: 978-1-56158-844-2 (alk. paper)

 ISBN-10: 1-56158-844-X (alk. paper)

 1. Prefabricated houses. 2. Modular coordination (Architecture) 3. House construction. 4. Architecture, Domestic. I. Title.

TH4819.P7K66 2007

643'.2--dc22

                                          2006021975

Printed in Singapore

10 9 8 7 6 5 4 3 2 1

The following manufacturers/names appearing in *Prefabulous* are trademarks: Cambria®; Carderock®; Cultured Stone®; Decra®; Galvalum®; GeoDeck™; Hardiplank®; Hearth & Home Technologies™; Lincoln Logs®; Myson®; Owens Corning®; Pella®; Richlite®; Solarcrete™; Styrofoam™; Teragren™; WeatherBest®; Wicanders®; Zincalume®

For Rob, with love

Acknowledgments

When I begin a project like this one, I begin by looking for exceptional homes. But what stays with me at the end of each book are the exceptional people I meet during the process—the homeowners, architects, manufacturers, builders, suppliers, and experts—whom I have come to know and now consider friends. I am grateful to all of these busy folks who took the time to talk at length and answer a multitude of questions.

As a result of this book, I now can keep abreast of happenings on Daufuskie Island thanks to Catherine Tillman and her newsletter, *The Front Porch*. And I have a new appreciation of traditional Australian architecture compliments of Peter Skinner at the University of Queensland and William Gunnar, who descends from a key figure in Australia's independence. Many of these people have embellished my life, and I am appreciative for having met them.

As always I am so grateful to my husband and children, who support all of my writing and now know much more about home construction than any of them needs to.

My friends are a continuous source of support, and I am so appreciative of them all.

It was a pleasure to work with The Taunton Press books group: Steve Culpepper for encouraging this project and seeing it through, Katie Benoit for all of her help, and Wendi Mijal for her great talent with both photographers and photography. Thanks also to Bridget Bradley for her editing.

My thanks to Dave Wrocklage, who was so supportive of this project, and to Eric Fulton for keeping me informed of industry information. Thank you to all of the photographers who did such a fine job of photographing the houses in this book. A special thank you to Mona Costa and Jim and Brett Mauri for their gracious help over and beyond. All of these people made it such fun to work on this book.

Contents

p 62

Foreward	3
Introduction	4
Modular	**22**
Moose Creek Lodge	28
Chez Poupon	34
Sunset Breezehouse	40
Maryfield House	46
Panelized	**52**
Coastal House	56
Greenridge House	62
Pfaff House	68
Structural Insulated Panels	**74**
Villa Kaki	78
Chaleff House	84
Timber Frame	**90**
Craftsman's Lodge	96
The Queenslander	102
House on the Saltwater Marsh	110
Bainbridge Island House	116
Hobbit Haven	122
Far Horizon Reflection Home	128

p 46

Introduction

I USED TO THINK THERE WAS ONLY ONE WAY
to build a house: A truck pulls up and unloads a pile of lumber and
then carpenters show up and start building—a process that, I know
from experience, can drag on for months.

Then a few years ago, a friend invited me to watch a crew "set" her
new modular house. I arrived that morning to an empty lot. By afternoon, the shell of the house was almost complete. The next day the
house was "buttoned up" weather tight, avoiding the moisture damage
that I'd dealt with on my own home construction.

Since then I've had the opportunity to see other types of prefab
houses going up. I'm always impressed by the accuracy of the construction, the speed with which it goes up, and the minimal waste, especially
compared with ordinary construction.
I've also learned that prefab means much
more than modular. Although modular—which are whole truck-size sections
built in a factory and shipped to a building
site (you've seen them on the highway)
—is a proportionally small percentage in
relation to overall construction, other
kinds of prefabrication are used in a
large number of homes built today.

Foreword

When I wrote *The Not So Big House* back in 1998 and included a section on panelization—the process I used to build my own house—little did I know that I'd be deluged with requests for more information about prefab houses. Over the past 10 years, there's been growing interest in off-site factory assembly of houses, generically referred to as "prefab," rather than stick-by-stick construction on site.

It has always amazed me that although we'd never agree to have a new car assembled in our driveway or a new dishwasher put together on our kitchen floor, for some reason many of us have no problem assuming that a house assembled on site is going to prduce a better quality product than one built in a factory. It just isn't so.

There are many benefits to assembling the components of a house in a controlled factory setting that's safe from the whims of Mother Nature. Not only can production proceed more efficiently, but the entire process can also be conducted in a more energy efficient and sustainable way, with all the wastc products recycled and reused. If you've ever driven by a typical construction site and raised an eyebrow at the dumpsters full of left-over materials, you'll quickly recognize that this new, prefabulous approach to house building is unquestionably a better way.

For some people, words like "modular," "manufactured," "panelized," and "prefabricated" conjure up visions of ticky-tacky subdivisions in which every house looks just the same. But the biggest story revealed in *Prefabuous* is that just because something is made in a factory doesn't mean it has to be boring or the same as hundreds of other houses. All the homes you'll see in the pages that follow are spectacular examples of what we'd normally call custom design. They *are* custom designed, but that tailoring does not preclude their being made using newer, more sustainable assembly practices. Prefab is definitely an idea whose time has come, and this is the book that tells us how to make it happen.

Sarah Susanka
Raleigh, North Carolina
January 2007

p 116

p 62

p 148

Log Construction 136

Idaho Chalet 142

Crooked Pine Ranch 148

Triple Run 154

Country Dream House 162

Gallatin River House 168

Concrete 176

Smith House 182

Jesse Road House 188

Steel 192

Lumley House 196

House on Patuxent River 202

Branford Point House 208

Resources 216

This mansion in Southampton, New York, is an excellent example of the beauty and sophistication that can now be obtained with modular construction.

Top photo by Kati and Max Mehlburger
Left photo by Ron Papageorge, Photographer

It is an amazing experience watching a modular unit being lifted with a crane and set on a foundation. Depending on the size and complexity of the house, often an entire structure can be set in a day. Photo courtesy Epoch Homes, Ltd.

While many of the earlier modular homes were labeled as bungalows, they now come in a variety of styles and can even have custom floor plans. Photo courtesy Quality Engineered Homes.

The Short History of Prefab

After seeking out other forms of prefab house construction, I started researching prefab systems to understand the varieties and their differences. There remains much confusion over the term "prefab" and its larger family of "building systems," which refer to all types of construction manufactured and assembled partially or entirely in a factory, plant, or yard.

As a concept, prefabrication isn't new. Factory-built houses in the United States date back to the catalog houses of the early 1900s. These houses gave a working family the opportunity to own a home at a reasonable cost, which was made possible by the mass construction of parts and bulk purchasing by the factories. Mail-order kit houses with all of the parts required to build the house were sold by companies such as Alladin Homes, Montgomery Ward, Bennett Homes, and Sears Roebuck and Company. The parts were produced in factories and shipped to the site, where the house was assembled by the homeowners or local builders. Most of the houses were labeled "bungalows," although they came in a variety of styles. Options such as paint color, type of wood trim, and door and cabinet design were selected in advance. Add-ons, such as porches and freestanding garages, were available for an extra fee.

Architects in the early 20th century, including such visionaries as Buckminster Fuller and Frank Lloyd Wright, began to experiment with prefabricated design. Although there was some public interest, people generally thought these houses looked boxy and odd. But by the 1950s, the prefab home industry had found its footing and began to focus on low-cost small houses rather than great design. It has only been in the last decade or two that architects, builders, and homeowners have begun to take advantage of what is called, in the industry, systems-built homes. Along the way, good design has crept back into the process. As you'll see in the pages to come, prefab is now much more than small and affordable.

Getting Bigger, Better, and More Custom

With demand increasing for customized designs, architects along with the industry are pushing the limits of what the public traditionally recognizes as prefab. They've also begun developing entirely new prefab

Kit houses bought from catalogs such as these were the forbearers of today's prefab houses. Photos courtesy The Clarke Library, Central Michigan University

This early example of a modular house is what many people still think of when they hear the word modular. Photo courtesy Epoch Homes, Ltd.

Rocio Romero, one of the architects forging new areas for prefab constructions, designed this modular house. Photo by Jennifer Watson/ Luminhaus

systems and combining existing ones in interesting new ways. For the first time, prefab houses are available that have custom floor plans, style, and rich detail—benefits not previously associated with prefab construction.

Combining custom appeal and attractive design with prefab's greater energy efficiency, lower construction waste, faster construction time, and better structural stability makes today's prefab home a better long-term investment for homeowners.

Homeowners seeking upscale homes are finding architects and manufacturers who will give them just what they want. Manufacturers now offer options, customize their stock house plans, and work closely with architects to expand their prefab designs.

In the past, builders were concerned about prefab's quality but generally were unfamiliar with the process. Once they realized it was fairly simple to transition from standard construction to prefab, more have explored the benefits of prefab construction.

The Systems

The most commonly used building systems are modular, panelized, log, timber frame, concrete, and steel frame. I include each system here, all of which are recognized by residential building codes. Structures such as manufactured homes or trailers, although they serve a purpose, are covered by a separate U.S. Department of Housing and Urban Development (HUD) code and are not included in this book.

Modular

Modular houses arrive on site the most complete of all prefab systems. Boxes, or modules, are engineered and assembled in a factory and shipped on trucks. Houses can be built with one module or dozens, in virtually any style. Built to endure the stresses of highway travel and being lifted with a crane, modulars contain up to 30 percent more building material than a comparable site-built home. When the drywall is hung, it is often glued as well as screwed to the wall studs.

It would be impossible to differentiate a modular house today from one that is built on site. Photo courtesy Epoch Homes, Ltd.

Structural insulated panels were used to build this beautiful house in Vermont. Photo courtesy Winterpanel

This house was built panelized to hasten construction during a cold Wisconsin winter. Photo courtesy Vetter Windows & Doors

This is a fast-growing business. The number of modular houses has nearly doubled in the last 10 years to approximately 206,000 in 2004, according to an industry report. In the last decade, a growing percentage of modular houses were custom designed, which makes them quite different from the modest homes that dominated the industry in its early days. And these custom-built modular houses are popping up in the most affluent areas.

Panelized

Probably the most widely used type of prefab is panelized construction. According to a study reported by *Automated Builder* magazine, panelized construction made up roughly 44 percent of single-family homes. For the study, panels included wood panels built with 2x4 lumber (in essence, traditionally framed wall, floor, and roof segments) and structural insulated panels (SIPs), which are sandwiches of foam insulation between two layers of plywood or similar sheet material. These panels are shipped to home sites where they are assembled like large three-dimensional puzzles.

Both types of panels are used to build entire houses and as infill for other systems such as timber frames or steel frames. To simplify the building process and cut down on construction time and labor, builders on site also use panelized components like floor, wall, ceiling, and roof trusses.

Photographed in 1940, this log cabin in Mercer County, Kentucky, is a good example of a typical early-American log home. The log homes built today have become more sophisticated in design, structure, and energy efficiency. Photo courtesy The Library of Congress

It is easy to see how log homes have evolved in the last 50 years. Photo by Roger Wade

The soaring ceilings in some timber-frame homes like this one add to the beauty and spaciousness of the house. One of the allures of this type of construction is the craftsmanship that can be seen in the frame itself. Photo courtesy Rich Frutchey Associates

Log

Log homes have come a long way from the one-room cabin days. Modern log houses are larger and better built, and most are built in a factory or "yard" and then assembled on site. Modern handling and cutting machinery make it more efficient to fabricate log homes in a factory setting. Today there are as many as 500 log-home manufacturers, accounting for an estimated 7 percent of custom home building.

In the mid 1980s, about 15,000 log homes were sold each year; today that figure has swelled to 26,000. Ten percent of the log homes are handcrafted, which means that logs are hewn and notched by hand. The other 90 percent use milled logs.

For homeowners, both the log-home tradition and the beauty of wood are the primary allure. A secondary advantage is that the wood's thickness and density, or thermal mass, make them energy efficient.

Timber frame

Timber-frame owners appreciate the traditional richness of the exposed beams and posts and the high, soaring ceilings, which are often features of timber-frame homes. Timber frames qualify as prefabricated because today most are built in a factory. Many are fabricated using sophisticated computer measuring and cutting equipment under controlled conditions.

According to the Timber Frame Business Council, more than 200 timber-frame companies do business in North America. To get a sense of its popularity, two national magazines are devoted to the topic, and about 12 annual timber frame and log shows are held each year.

This house was built with concrete walls and systems that make it energy efficient and strong. Photo courtesy Farr Associates

This beautiful waterfront house is a hybrid, with a steel frame and SIPs infills. It combines the strength of steel with the energy-efficiency of panels. Photo by Phillip Jensen-Carter

Concrete

Unlike in Europe, where concrete homes have been built for hundreds of years, concrete has rarely been used for residential construction in this country. In 1993 approximately 3 percent of the homes built in the United States used prefab concrete panels; today approximately 16 percent are built using some type of prefab concrete system.

Although concrete has typically been a more costly method of building, its popularity is growing because it is plentiful, easy to create in a variety of colors and in a multitude of forms, is virtually weatherproof and bugproof, and when reinforced with steel is strong enough to stand up to hurricanes, tornados, and earthquakes. In addition to all those benefits, concrete can be a very energy-efficient material for home construction.

Steel

Metal is one of the most recyclable building materials; it offers stability against hurricanes, earthquakes, and fire; and it eliminates concerns regarding termites and other pests. Steel is a practical alternative to wood because of its stability and longevity.

One reason steel frames have not been used for houses in the past has been in finding builders who can build with it. Today more and more companies in North America prefabricate the framing components for houses and can recommend qualified builders to erect them.

Hybrids

Many houses included in this book are hybrids, meaning that one house includes several different types of prefab construction. One house was built with a log "stack" and a timber frame with a panelized system infill. Another was built with a unique steel frame and infilled with SIPs. Advanced technology now being employed in factories has vastly expanded design and construction possibilities.

Reasons to Consider Prefab

Just as we read labels on the food we purchase to make sure it has healthy ingredients and shop for cars that are fuel efficient and safe, we look for the same high standards in our new houses. We want to live in a healthy environment with a minimum of toxic chemicals and that have limited potential for mold and mildew.

We also want a safe environment, with homes that are built to withstand insects, rot, and weather extremes. And now more than ever, there is concern for protecting the environment and slowing depletion of our natural resources.

A theme you'll see woven throughout this book is that of the homeowners, architects, and builders who were convinced that better ways existed to build houses. Instead of building the traditional way, they searched for a more energy-efficient and faster way to build. Most of the people whose homes you'll see are busy professionals. Yet they investigated and, in some cases, took the risk of employing these methods. The results include many houses that would be considered beautiful, some attractive and unique, but all energy efficient and eco-friendly in their own way.

This house was built with a combination of several systems including log construction, timber frame, and panelized sections used for infill. Photo by Karl Neumann, Neumann Photography, Inc.

This book takes a look at the marvelous variety of building systems, shows the results, and explores the unique set of circumstances and conditions that produced these homes. And although each house looks different from the others, all were manufactured partially or almost completely in a controlled factory environment and then erected on site.

When you listen to architects, to people in the business, and to the homeowners, you'll know that prefabrication is the way houses of the future will be built. Every year brings an increase in the sophistication of the materials, the energy efficiency of the materials and construction methods, and the design options that are possible.

Each house was manufactured in a completely controlled factory environment.

People are choosing prefab methods to keep to their budgets; to make it easier to estimate the costs of materials and labor; to reduce energy costs and construction time; and to create a healthier environment, inside the home and outside, through reduction of construction waste.

Prefab: Built Strong

Houses can quickly be reduced to rubble in a matter of minutes when fierce storms and hurricanes hit. In some cases, of course, nothing can endure the ferocity of Mother Nature, but there is evidence that many factory-built homes survived in a storm's high winds when traditionally constructed homes all around them were destroyed.

For instance, a number of modular houses withstood a hurricane's 110-mile-per-hour winds while houses around them were destroyed. In 1992, after Hurricane Andrew's category 4 winds blew through Florida,

the Federal Emergency Management Agency reported that modular homes "provided an inherently rigid system that performed much better than conventional residential framing."

Because modular houses are built in a factory, they are more rigidly inspected and often overbuilt to ensure strength. The Timber Framers Guild of North America reports on timber-frame homes that have survived when other houses around them have been destroyed. In 1985, a tornado wiped out whole towns in northwestern Pennsylvania. A timber-frame home in the area was lifted 3 in. off its foundation and its roof blew away, but the frame and most of the house was intact.

Some systems-built houses are also safer from wildfires. Concrete, for example, doesn't disintegrate unless exposed to thousands of degrees Fahrenheit—more than is typical in a common house fire. Although metal will melt at high temperatures, it will not burn and, if properly finished, is another excellent alternative in fire-prone areas.

Conserving Resources

Homeowners are more conscious than ever of the demands put on the environment by their choices of building materials and the vast amount of waste home building generates. Just drive past a residential development under construction and count the number of dumpsters.

In 1994, more than 1.4 million single-family homes were built at an average size of 2,300 sq. ft. For a sense of the waste involved, consider that 8,000 pounds of waste ends up in a landfill from the construction of one 2,000-sq.-ft. home. Constructing all or parts of a house in a factory setting dramatically decreases construction waste. According to a study by the Wood Truss Council of America, a typical panelized home used 13 yards less lumber than a stick-built home.

Waste is not only reduced in a factory setting, but the waste that is generated is often recycled. In modular construction, waste from drywall is returned to the manufacturer, while sawdust and leftover wood, called offcuts, are sometimes used to heat the factory. Short cuts of wood are used on other projects. In fact, most wooden trusses are

These trees burned in the October 2004 Power Fire in Amador County, California, are examples of standing dead trees that can be used to build prefabricated homes. Photo courtesy California Forest Foundation

made with these small offcuts "finger-jointed" together to create a structural member that's stronger than a piece of solid wood.

Other systems such as SIPs utilize engineered wood that, when bonded to foam cores, creates a wall that has greater energy efficiency and more structural integrity than a typical plywood-sheathed house. The log and timber industry uses recycled timbers and standing dead trees. Removing standing dead trees is also good for the forest, ridding the landscape of a safety or fire hazard and allowing new trees ample resources to grow.

The Accuracy of Prefab

Machinery used in prefabrication factories, in addition to conserving materials, is more accurate and efficient than ever. Computer-controlled saws make multiple cuts in wood with one pass, saving time and labor. Sophisticated machinery such as CNC machines (see the photo on the facing page) are directed by computers to determine the materials needed, enabling the manufacturer to better plan the use of raw materials.

Such large equipment would be out of the question on a construction site. Computer programs used to design the houses also manage the measuring and materials cutting so parts are cut accurately with a minimum of waste and pieces fit together easily on site, making the assembly time efficient as well.

CNC machines are commonly used in factories that build prefab-ricated houses, increasing the accuracy of the construction and hastening the production time.
Photo courtesy Hundegger USA

The Economics of Prefab

Greater energy efficiency

Many of the systems described in this book, such as concrete, will endure all types of climates and weather for years with little mainte-nance or repair. Modular and panelized building present an economic advantage because factory construction reduces labor costs and waste.

The cost of removing material waste from the job site is also sub-stantially reduced with prefabrication. One of the builders I met while writing this book told me that he needs no dumpsters for the panelized homes he builds, which saves him thousands in rental and hauling fees. For each standard home he constructs, the builder needs at least five dumpsters.

Other systems such as concrete and SIPs save money over time with lower heating and cooling costs. SIPs, which have uninterrupted continuous insulation, decrease heat loss. The high thermal mass (or density) of logs and concrete reduces heating and cooling costs. Systems that don't have the advantage of thermal mass, such as modular and panelized, have found products and methods of construction that make houses more efficient and bring down energy costs.

Designed to look like an old barn, this timber frame was infilled with SIPs. Photo courtesy Winterpanel and Ted Benson

Modular components are being transported to Daufuskie Island to be set. Photo by Steve Basset, Haven Homes Southeast

When energy efficiency goes up, other costs go down: There is a reduced cost for heating and cooling equipment because such a house needs a smaller furnace and air-conditioning unit. Depending on the type of system and the location of the house, equipment and labor savings can range up to 15 percent annually over conventional construction.

The building industry is continually working to develop greener, healthier, and more efficient products. Many of the systems-built homes today exceed the federal EPA's Energy Star requirements.

Shortage of skilled labor

The shortage of skilled construction labor is a growing concern. Most high schools have either eliminated or cut back on shop programs, where once students first acquired building skills. And working conditions in the construction industry, which is done in all climates and in all weather, discourages many from the home-building profession.

However, with factory construction, much of the work is done in a comfortable and controlled environment. The work is steady and predictable and the income less susceptible to disruption from weather conditions.

Systems-built homes also make sense in areas where qualified labor is scarce or expensive. Homes are being barged to islands like Daufuskie Island in South Carolina or Nantucket in Massachusetts, where labor is expensive; to backwoods locations, where labor is scarce; and to dense urban areas, where the reduced on-site construction time has less impact on neighbors.

Saving time

An advantage often expressed by owners of systems-built homes is shorter construction time. People want to be inconvenienced for the shortest possible time and want to keep the costs of temporary housing down as much as possible.

And because of production speed, the time required to carry a construction loan is shorter, which allows homeowners to lock in a mortgage rate sooner. A site-built home may take as long as two years to complete, whereas some prefab homes can be completed in only months.

Better warranties

With any house, problems occur from time to time. Minor leaks occur, plaster cracks, a window or roof leaks, and mechanical systems such as furnaces, boilers, and compressors don't always work as they are supposed to.

With stick-built homes, local builders usually offer a 1-year warranty. Many systems manufacturers offer longer warranties; modular manufacturers, for example, offer a 10-year limited warranty on their houses.

Part of the allure of a log cabin is the cozy feeling of the wood beams on the exterior and a warm fire in the fireplace. Photo by Roger Wade

Modular

Breckenridge, CA | 2,600 sq. ft.

Grouse Creek Lodge

Watching a modular house being "set" is a spectacular sight. An entire house, or large section, is lifted, carried through the air, and set down on a prepared foundation. In one or two days a nearly complete house sits where none existed. Although an increasing number of modular houses are popping up around the country, it is still a relatively new concept. We have all seen the large modules traveling the highway on flatbed trucks. Unless you observe a modular house actually being set, you wouldn't know from the finished house that it had arrived in pieces.

Chez Poupon

Quogue, NY | 8,000 sq. ft. p 34

Maryfield House

Daufuskie Island, SC | 2,900 sq. ft. p 46

Sunset Breezehouse

Menlo Park, CA | 1,800 sq. ft. p 40

23

When the modules arrive at the construction site, they are typically installed in one or two days, depending on the size of the house. A module is lifted with a crane and set on the prepared foundation.
Photo courtesy Epoch Homes

Modular houses are composed of one or more modules that are factory built, transported by truck, and set on a foundation. Modular houses can be two modules, such as the Sunset Breeze-house (see p. 40), or grand, such as Chez Poupon (see p. 34), which was 15 boxes. Modular houses can be built in any style. Even a log cabin can be built in modules (see p. 28). Some people use the manufacturers' designs; others have the company customize those plans; still others prefer to hire their own architect.

Modular houses used to be perceived as cheap, hardly an improvement over a mobile home. But as design and construction improved, the trend has been toward custom homes that are larger and more architecturally interesting. This improved quality has resulted in more people choosing modular. In 1994, 109,000 modular houses were built in the United States. By 2004, the number had almost doubled to 206,000, according to an industry journal.

Modules are transported from factories around the country over local roads and highways to the construction site. **Photo courtesy Epoch Homes**

This massive house was delivered to the site with 15 modules. Whereas some houses are delivered somewhat complete, much of the work on the Chez Poupon was completed on site. Photo by Ron Papageorge

Saving Money

Modular companies purchase materials in bulk, and savings are passed on to the consumer. Factories generally are located in areas with low labor costs, and money saved on labor further brings down costs. They're also faster. The less time it takes to build, the lower the labor costs and the less time the homeowner must carry a construction loan.

Saving Time

Time is another factor. Most modular houses can be built in seven to ten days, set in a day or two, and completed in as fast as three weeks.

Saving the Environment

An unseen advantage of modular houses less construction waste. At the end of a standard house construction, dumpsters are filled with waste.

Indistinguishable from a traditionally built log home, this house was set over a weekend and completed in several weeks. Photo courtesy Quality Engineered Homes, Ltd.

The Sunset Breezehouse has been designed to be particularly environmentally friendly, with sustainable and energy efficient elements. Photo by Tom Story/Sunset Magazine

Modular units are lifted by a crane and set on the foundation.

Construction of an average 2,000-sq.-ft. house produces 8,000 pounds and 20 cubic yards of waste.

In a factory, wood building materials are recycled, either by using them on other houses or for burning to heat the factory.

Remote and Distant Locations

In remote locations or on islands accessible only by boat, such as the Daufuskie Island house (see p. 46), it is often difficult to find builders. Suitable materials may also be inaccessible or expensive because of transportation costs, making it often easier to transport modules than to build from scratch.

In a second-home situation, the homeowner may not be available at the construction site on a day-to-day basis to make last-minute design decisions. With a modular house, those decisions are made before the start of construction.

Built to Last

The most up-to-date equipment is used to cut and assemble wall, floor, and roof sections, which are assembled on large horizontal frames to ensure flat and level surfaces.

For standard houses, most homeowners get a one- or two-year warranty. Many modular houses come with a 10-year warranty. Modular houses are built to comply with national building codes. Inspectors visit

The lot around this traditionally built house demonstrates the debris that can be created and the disturbance to the neighborhood when a house is built on site.

Prefabricated architectural enhancements like these dormers are shipped separately and installed after the house is set. Other enhancements include reverse gables, bumpouts, and angled bays. Photo Courtesy Epoch Homes

the factory and perform code-compliance checks. Some modular houses are built to exceed local structural requirements, such as the Sunset Breezehouse (see p. 40).

Poised to Grow

Modular construction is growing rapidly. Although it's in its infancy, the industry will spawn new modular factories to serve locations where it is currently difficult to get modular homes.

Designers and builders are now using timber-frame and log construction in their modular homes to add to the design options. This hybrid segment continues to evolve. For instance, structural insulated panels (see pp. 74–77) are now being used to create the outer walls in some modular homes to make them more energy efficient.

Good sources of information are the Modular Building Systems Association at www.modularhousing.com and the National Association of Home Builder's Building System Council at www.buildingsystems.org.

Building houses in a controlled factory environment offers better quality and faster construction time. Modular companies can build 5 to 15 houses a week, like this one in New Hampshire, where modules move along tracts at a rapid pace as parts of the units are completed. Photo Courtesy Epoch Homes

In some locations, such as Martha's Vineyard and Daufuskie Island, it is easier to transport the modules by barge than to find the craftsmen and materials to build the house on site. Photo courtesy Epoch Homes

Moose Creek Lodge

Manufacturer
American
Timbercraft

Location
Breckenridge, CO

Square Footage
2,600 Sq. Ft

Photography
Randy O'Rourke
except where noted

THE TIME AND EXPENSE OF BUILDING A HOME is enough to scare some people away from the idea altogether. Tom and Kris Chiapete had basically given up on their dream of building a mountain log cabin after hearing about the two-year process their friends went through. Luckily, Tom found a solution while searching the Internet that would solve their scheduling and financial concerns—a company that builds modular log homes.

With newfound enthusiasm, the Chiapetes purchased property for their modular log home on a wooded site in Breckenridge, Colorado. Tom found a floor plan on the Internet that he liked and submitted it to American Timbercraft, who helped the Chiapetes adapt it to their needs. The Chiapetes wanted their house to emulate the style of the Lincoln Logs® toys that their children once played with, and so chose brown stained logs and a green asphalt roof.

Their initial concern about the time involved with building a house was more than solved by modular construction. They placed their order in May, and the modules were delivered in August. The modules arrived with windows, roofing, kitchen cabinets, appliances, and fire-

This modular log home is indistinguishable from a traditionally built one. Photo at left courtesy American Timbercraft

The sections arrive by flatbed trucks the morning of the set (top left). The foundation is ready for the modulars to be set (middle left). The first box is set in place (bottom left). A roof unit is being set (top right). At the end of the day, the house is set (bottom right).

Photos this page courtesy American Timbercraft

place installed and was set over a weekend. Even the porches and decks were prebuilt. After the modules were set, they only needed to hook up the radiant-heating system, connect plumbing, wiring, and sewer lines, and trim the module seams. The Chiapetes were able to move in a couple of weeks later.

Built to Last

The Chiapetes' house is Western style and built with lodge pole pine standing-dead timbers (see the sidebar on the facing page). The logs have a Swedish cope profile, which is notched so that one log fits tightly to ones below and above. The corners are saddle notched (see the sidebar on p. 170), which is another way to lock logs together.

Standing Dead Trees

It's not uncommon to see dead trees still standing in the forest after being killed by fire, insects, or lightning. Although they're quite dead, their wood—at least for a while—is perfectly fine and, depending on the amount of time the tree has stood, the wood is often dry and good for building.

Log home builders and timber framers have long recognized the usefulness of these trees for home construction. Depending on the length of time since the tree died, they are often much drier than freshly cut trees and so have undergone much of the shrinkage that takes place as wood loses moisture.

The species of wood most often used as standing dead are Douglas fir, western white pine, and ponderosa pine.

The Chiapetes enjoy relaxing on their porch and looking out at the wooded view.

The Chiapetes selected their green kitchen cabinets at a local branch of a national hardware retailer. This made it easier for American Timbercraft, at a distance away, to purchase exactly what the customers wanted.

First Floor

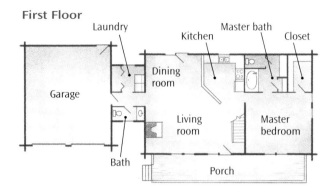

- Laundry
- Kitchen
- Master bath
- Closet
- Garage
- Dining room
- Bath
- Living room
- Master bedroom
- Porch

Second Floor

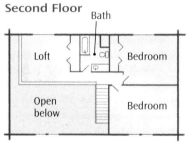

- Bath
- Loft
- Bedroom
- Open below
- Bedroom

Jack Nipko, founder of American Timbercraft, has patented his type of modular construction. He says his houses have to be strong to withstand being picked up and moved to remote home sites over often unpaved roads and rocky terrain.

Nipko's inspiration came from his early experience building log homes the old-fashioned way—on site and one log at a time. He was frustrated with the time lost traveling into town several times a day to pick up supplies and the difficulty of getting subcontractors to a remote site. He decided there had to be a better way. Building modules in a factory where materials and reliable labor are close at hand and protected from the elements was the answer.

Kris says her modular house has the special quality she expected, which is the beauty and warmth of the logs. "Everybody that sees the house is surprised when we tell them it was shipped in seven pieces," she says.

Whenever they visit their Breckenridge home, the Chiapetes enjoy entertaining family and friends at their rustic dining table.

The loft sitting area is a great place to read a book, watch television, or take a nap after a long day of skiing (left).

The staircase and railing were fabricated in the American Timbercraft facility and connected on site.

American Timbercraft installed the gas stone fireplace in its factory, then the gas lines were connected once the house was set.

Chez Poupon

Architect
Mike Gentile

Manufacturer
Haven Homes

Builder
Barry Altman,
The Builder, Inc.

Location
Quogue, NY

Square Footage
8,000 Sq. Ft

Photography
Ron Papageorge
except where noted

BARRY ALTMAN HAS BEEN BUILDING MODULAR homes for more than 20 years, including one that he built for himself, his wife Marcia, and their children. About five years ago, he purchased six acres in Quogue, a quiet and beautiful section of the Hamptons in Long Island, with the idea of subdividing it into three homesteads. He planned to build two houses on spec and keep the third lot for himself for a new family house.

Once they decided to build in Quogue, Barry asked Marcia to come up with a design. Marcia started with the floor plan of their current home and added a dining room, larger kitchen, a back stairway, and additional bedrooms. Working with other modular plans she had access to, she finished the layout for the new house and hired architect Mike Gentile to create the drawings and ensure the plans met local code requirements.

After months of planning, Barry ordered the house from Haven Homes. Unlike most modular houses, which are delivered nearly complete, this one only included framing, insulation, drywall, some wiring, and some plumbing. Finish materials, including doors, windows, roofing, fireplaces, moldings, and trim,

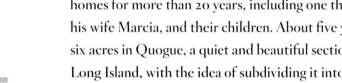

34

Passersby would never imagine that this mansion was delivered in parts on a flatbed truck and assembled on site (above). All of the siding, roofing, windows, and doors were installed on site after the modulars, or boxes, were set (left). Photo at left by Sheri Koones

A checkerboard pattern of grass and stone leads up to a handcrafted mahogany entry door. The unique pathway was inspired by those Marcia saw in Europe and in magazines over the years.

were installed on site. Some architectural features were preformed in a factory, such as the coffered ceiling (see the sidebar on p. 39) in the media room, but finished and installed on site. Despite all the on-site work that was done, having much of the house built in modules cut the construction time from about two years to ten months. "The best part of modular construction is the ability to control the schedule and the quality of the construction," Marcia says.

Style and Substance

The Altmans wanted what Marcia calls a "mod-iterranean" style, one that incorporates the best qualities of an old Mediterranean home with the newest modern features and systems for creating a comfortable lifestyle. After traveling in the south of France many times over the past 20 years, the Altmans had become very fond of Mediterranean style. Like many homeowners who want to deviate from the prevailing style

The pool house includes a bathroom, shower, dressing room, mini-kitchen, and a sitting area for escaping the hot summer sun. The swimming pool has integrated speakers for music that can only be heard under the water and at the shallow end.

of an area—which in the Hamptons is Shingle Style—the Altmans had some difficulty convincing the local architectural design review board that their home would enhance the neighborhood. Their plans were ultimately approved and their home is now well regarded in the area and is an amazement to people when they learn that it's modular.

Many parts of the house were handmade by craftsmen to emulate old European designs. For example, the custom wrought-iron railings in the entry hall, the balcony grills, and upper-floor window grills were modeled after Art Deco French grillwork.

The mahogany windows and doors were inspired by those Marcia and Barry had seen in French homes and hotels they had stayed in over the years. A millwork craftsman in Pennsylvania traveled five hours each week to deliver the doors and windows as he completed them so Barry could stay on schedule. The decorative board-and-batten-style shutters were also fashioned to look like Mediterranean.

First Floor

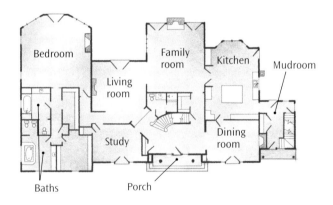

Second Floor

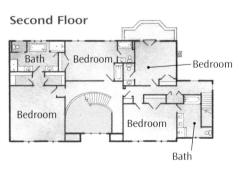

The rear of the house is the perfect place for outdoor summer entertaining with a 30-ft. by 50-ft. pool, a competition-size tennis court, and a pool house. The mahogany doors open to a spacious patio where a built-in barbecue is used to prepare meals.

Antique tumbled marble is used throughout this gracious entry hall (right).

These beautiful mahogany windows in an upstairs bathroom open up to a view of the pool, pool house, and garden (below).

The kitchen, like the house, is a wonderful combination of old world charm and modern convenience. Ceiling beams are made of roughsawn cedar stained a dark mahogany color. All of the fixtures—including the warming drawer, two dishwashers, sinks, and pot filler above the six-burner cooktop—make it easy to entertain large groups.

Fond of mustard tones (hence the name Chez Poupon), Marcia carried them throughout the interior in furnishings, walls, and in the stucco exterior. She added a number of bright colors as well. The house is furnished with a mixture of antiques and modern pieces. Marcia researched fabrics on the Internet and put together story boards for each room. She and Barry collected many items while traveling through Europe and kept them in storage until the house was complete.

The Altmans picked up this colorful chandelier hanging over the breakfast area on one of their trips to Murano, an island off the coast of Venice.

Coffered Ceilings

Coffered ceilings have recessed square panels and are bordered with ornamental trim. They are often used in dens or libraries and can have elaborate moldings, as in the Altman house, or simple designs. By using different moldings, coffered ceilings can take on the look of a variety of architectural styles including Arts and Crafts, contemporary, or Victorian. The square panels can be made out of stucco, marble, brick, plaster, drywall, or wood, which was used in the Altman media room.

The Altmans created a large formal dining room for holiday dinners and other gatherings. The shape of the tray ceiling is repeated on the floor with a chevron design in wide oak planks. The unusual sideboard with a handpainted palm tree motif was made for the Altmans in Florida. They often open the double elliptical doors to a small marble patio that overlooks the front lawn and gardens.

Sunset Breezehouse

Architectural Team
Michelle Kaufmann Designs:
Michelle Kaufman,
Scott Landry,
Dan Gregory,
Peter O. Whiteley

Manufacturer
Britco Structures, Ltd

Builder
DeMattei Construction, Inc.

Interior Designer
Yvonne Stender

Location
Menlo Park, CA

MICHELLE KAUFMANN BEGAN DESIGNING modular houses when she and her husband, Kevin Cullen, were considering building their own house. Michelle wanted an economical house that could be built quickly, while Kevin wanted the house to be eco-friendly. Her first modular design, the Glidehouse, met their requirements. The Glidehouse was such an enormous success that *Sunset* magazine asked Kaufmann to join them in designing a second modular home. The result of that partnership is the Sunset Breezehouse.

Like her previous design, Kaufmann chose to "create a home design that embraced the environment and was an alternative to the inwardly focused McMansions." Kaufmann's designs are influenced by her upbringing in Iowa, where she observed the way farm buildings incorporate many sustainable elements. They use durable, low-maintenance materials, and their layout and window placement take advantage of breezes that can cool on hot days.

Kaufmann designed the Breezehouse for casual indoor-outdoor living in which garden areas would be connected to the bedrooms, master bath, entryway, and kitchen. One of the most innovative features of the house is the "breezespace," which

The breezehouse side module during construction in the factory (top left). The roof modules are being set with the crane (bottom left). The front elevation of the Sunset Breezehouse (above). Photo above by Tom Story, Sunset Magazine; Photos at left by Michelle Kaufmann Designs

With glass doors opening up the corners of the bedroom, the interior space is blended with the exterior garden (right). **Photo by Michelle Kaufmann Designs**

The courtyards open to the interior breezespace, blurring the boundary between the interior and exterior (below). **Photo by Tom Story, Sunset Magazine**

is a glass-enclosed breezeway in the center of the house covered by a butterfly-shaped roof. Walls of glass fold like accordions to open up the breezeway to the house. The space functions as the main living and dining area. It is flanked by the kitchen and second bedroom in one wing and the flexible library/guest room/office and master bedroom on the other side.

Custom Choices and Finishes

Most modular designs can be customized to a degree, which Kaufmann had been doing to Glidehouse designs. But she soon discovered that to take full advantage of factory production, she would have to limit customization and offer a selection of configurations and materials. Although options are limited, a homeowner can still get an individualized Breezehouse design. They can choose from one of several different roof configurations, from a variety of positions for the side modules (which can be parallel, perpendicular, or slanted), and from several types of exterior siding, including wood, cement board, and steel. They also can pick whether they want a two-, three-, or four-bedroom home.

Kaufmann also offers a complete package of interior options in her modular homes, including paint, flooring, faucets, and other finishes.

The Buying Process

Once a buyer selects the design and layout and orders the home, they simply wait for the house to be delivered. Site-built homes require much more time and frequently include a number of change orders and progress meetings. The Breezehouse can be delivered about six months after the order is placed. It arrives 90 percent complete, with walls painted, floors and cabinets installed, and wiring, plumbing, and heating coils built in. The house can be set in two days. Once utility lines are hooked up and glass walls installed, it takes just four to six more weeks until the homeowners can move in.

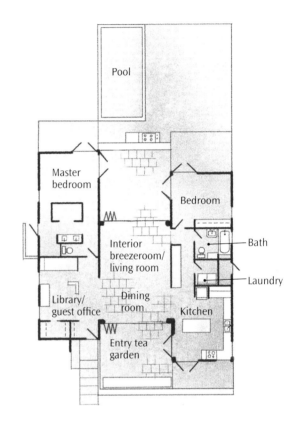

The kitchen has cherry cabinets and windows carefully located to direct light on the work surfaces of recycled paper countertops (Richlite). Photo by Michelle Kaufmann Designs

Folding Glass Doors

The glass doors that flank the breezeway in Sunset Breezehouse are called NanaWalls. When closed, they look like solid floor-to-ceiling windows and provide an acoustic barrier. But a hidden track-and-roller system allows the entire wall to be opened. The windows disappear, bringing the outdoors in with an unobstructed view.

Panels up to 26 ft. wide stow neatly to the side. Flush-floor and raised-track designs are available depending on weather conditions, available overhang, and drainage. Frames are available in aluminum, wood, and wood-clad aluminum. Many configurations are offered for interior or exterior use, including straight track, right angles, and curves. NanaWalls also comes in a model that is certified by Dade County, Florida, for use in hurricane zones. Photo by Michelle Kaufmann Designs

Environmentally Friendly

Kaufmann has always been concerned about sustainable design and incorporates it into her plans. In the Breezehouse, she uses cross-ventilation for cooling and stone tiles that act as a thermal mass to absorb heat during the day and radiate it back at night. Windows, clerestories, and skylights maximize natural light and ventilation and minimize the need for artificial lighting. The breezespace roof unobtrusively supports optional solar panels and screens glare. Eco-friendly options available are no-VOC (volatile organic compound) paints, kitchen and bathroom countertops made of Richlite® (a recycled paper product), and bamboo flooring, which is a highly sustainable product.

Although the prototype Sunset Breezehouse is built to suit a moderate climate, Kaufmann can alter the design for colder climates by reducing the amount of glass in the breezespace or adding insulated panels that slide to cover the glass walls. If built in a heavy snow area, "we would increase the structural sizing and spacing to handle larger snow loads, and slope the side module roofs to allow the snow to slide off," Kaufmann says.

The butterfly-type roof allows solar panels to be screened from the view of adjacent houses. Photo by Michelle Kaufmann Designs

The office-type workstation, conveniently located off the kitchen, was created by widening the hallway and adding skylights. Photo by Michelle Kaufmann Designs

NanaWall glass doors slide to one side to open the breezespace to one or both courtyards. Photo by Tom Story, Sunset Magazine

Maryfield House

Architectural Company
Hall & Hall Architects

Manufacturer
Nationwide Homes, Inc.

Builder
Jack Harris, Daufuskie Holdings, Inc.

Location
Daufuskie Island, SC

Square Footage
2,900 Sq. Ft

Photography
Chipper Hatter

CATHERINE TILLMAN KNEW THAT SOMEDAY she would have a yellow summer house at the beach with a tin roof, picket fence, and porch. The yellow house remained just a dream until Catherine and her husband David took a short trip to South Carolina's Daufuskie Island, which Catherine knew as the island described as Yamacraw Island in one of her favorite books, *The Water Is Wide* by Pat Conroy. While touring the island, Catherine found the yellow house.

They bought the yellow house but, unfortunately, after enjoying it just one summer, it burned to the ground while they were home in Atlanta. That spurred them to rebuild the house, bigger and better than the old. And they planned to make it their year-round home rather than a getaway. The only concern was its island location, which would make it difficult and expensive to construct. But after visiting a modular house on the island, they got in touch with the designers, Hall & Hull Architects.

The original house that sat on the property burned down. The new house was placed on the lot in a different position than the old house so that it could be framed by the trees and the owners would have a more expansive front yard (top).

Starting Over

Because it was important to them that their house have an authentic "low country" feel, the Tillmans spent weeks with the architects working out details. And although they were committed to build modular, at the time it was difficult to find a modular company that would build to their requirements. That led them to build the lower floor of the house using modular and the upper floor, roof, and porch using standard construction. Now, of course, companies will build a house to an entirely custom design.

Antique wicker furniture adorns this expansive front section of the porch.

The downstairs office/den looks out over a screened-in section of the porch that the owners hope to make a sleeping porch someday with a large swing for napping. For now, guests can have a private breakfast here among the rich foliage. Like most of the doors in the house, these French doors have transoms to flood the house with light.

The modular sections were delivered to the island by barge six weeks after they were ordered and set in one day. If the entire structure had been built from modular units, it would have taken about six months to complete rather than the 12 months it took to add the standard-construction second floor and roof.

As is often the case during home construction, there were good days and bad. An example of the bad was the day it rained during construction of the upper floor and the drywall in the modular units below was damaged. If Catherine were ever to build on the island again, the house would be completely modular. It is too difficult and costly to barge supplies to the island, and contractors have to travel by ferry from Savannah and Hilton Head.

The Tillmans' modules were delivered with built-in cabinets and part of the staircase already installed, but much of the interior and exterior finish work was completed on site, including installation of the fiber-cement siding, broad pine plank floors, moldings, and kitchen appliances.

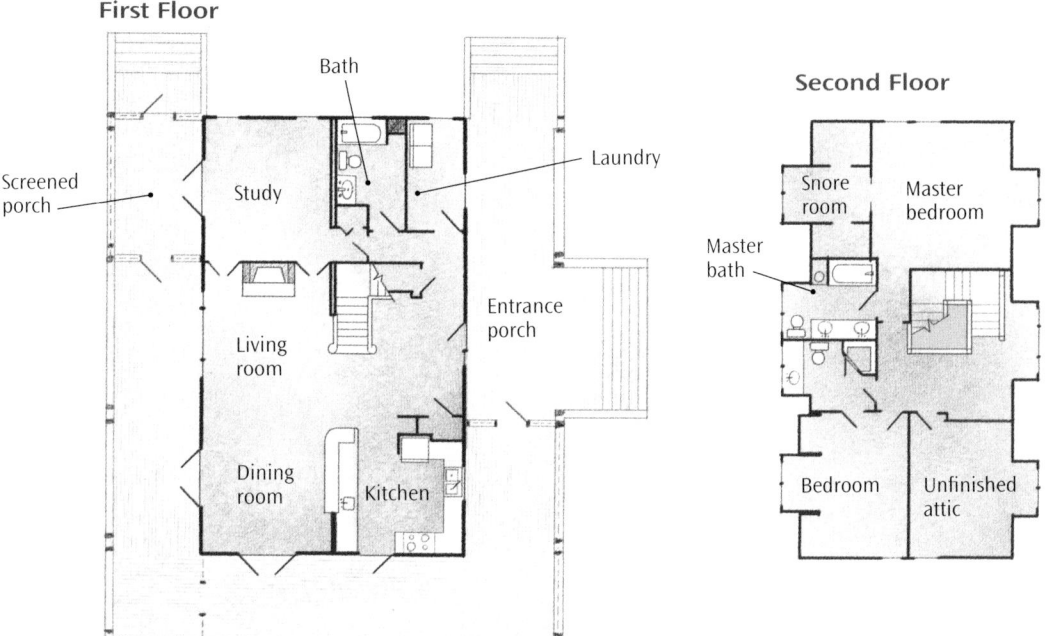

First Floor

Screened porch

Bath

Study

Laundry

Living room

Entrance porch

Dining room

Kitchen

Second Floor

Snore room

Master bedroom

Master bath

Bedroom

Unfinished attic

The lower portion of the staircase was built in the modular factory and the top portion was built on site. In the entry is an antique "hall tree," which Catherine takes with her wherever she lives.

Daufuskie Island

Daufuskie Island sits halfway between Hilton Head and Tybee islands. Just 2½ miles wide by 5 miles long, the island is accessible only by ferry. There are no traffic lights, no grocery stores, and mostly unpaved roads, which are part of its charm.

For groceries, residents take a ferry, pick up their car in Hilton Head, drive to the store, and back again. Luckily, there are two restaurants on the island and a small general store.

Residents can use the private ferry owned by the Daufuskie Island Resort and Breathe Spa at certain times of the day. There is one gated community on the island and two other communities currently under development. The rest of the island is referred to as the Historic District, which is several small neighborhoods including the Maryfield section, where the Tillmans live.

In this upstairs guest bedroom a drape was used instead of a closet door, bringing a touch of low country style to the room. The antique washstand now serves as a table; it is one of the many items throughout the house that Catherine has collected over the years.

They topped off the house with a standing-seam metal roof, which was part of Catherine's dream house because she loves the sound it makes when it rains.

When Catherine's second child went off to college, she and David moved to Daufuskie Island for good. These days, Catherine keeps island residents abreast of local news in her monthly newsletter, *The Front Porch*. Naturally, the Tillmans use their porch all the time. Neighbors often comment that it is the greatest porch—with a house attached—that they have ever seen.

The bunk beds and window seat were built into the room for the Tillmans' two daughters. The girls decorated their room using as much color as possible.

Beadboard, which is typically low country style, extends two-thirds of the way up the wall, adding architectural detail to this bathroom. The small shelf above stores small collectibles (above).

The pillar to the right of the cabinets indicates the "marriage wall" between the two modular boxes. One box includes the dining room, living room, and den and the other the kitchen, foyer, laundry room, and bathroom.

Panelized

Panelized construction is a fast-growing method of building used in about 30 percent of North American houses today. Wall, floor, and roof components made out of 2x4 panels are prefabricated in a factory, numbered for assembly, and trucked to the home site to be erected.

The earliest panels came with both siding and drywall. But because building codes required electrical inspections, manufacturers had to leave the panel interiors open so the wiring chases could be inspected. It is also now rare to see exterior siding on panels, though they do normally include wood sheathing. Some manufacturers install windows and doors; others leave them for site installation.

Coastal House

p 56

Annapolis, MD | 6,372 sq. ft.

p 68

Point Richmond, CA | 3,600 sq. ft.

p 62

Lake Geneva, WI | 7,100 sq. ft.

Traditional framing techniques are used in this panelized factory, except that walls are built on a specialized framing table instead of on the ground. Materials are stored and components constructed in ideal conditions. Photo courtesy Sterling Building Systems

Panels can be used for framing or for filling in the walls of a timber frame. The Coastal House (see p. 56) is an example of panelization with timber frames. The Greenridge and Pfaff houses (see pp. 62 and 68) are examples of purely panelized construction.

And panels do not limit the house design. They can be built in any style and with any roofing and siding. When the house is complete, it looks like any other.

Cost-Saving Aspects

A 1996 study showed two houses erected side by side—one built with conventional materials and the other built with prefabricated wood trusses and wall panels. The prefabricated materials were initially more costly than the conventional house ($14,457 vs. $12,928), but after labor and cleanup costs, the panelized house was $3,356 less expensive. The prefabricated house was also completed in 253 fewer hours, at a savings of $4,560.

Time-Saving Aspects

The faster a builder can build a house the better he is financially. Speed is also an advantage to the homeowner, who has a shorter construction loan. In the case of the Pfaff House (see p. 68), panels allowed the owner to finish the house quickly in time to meet a bank deadline.

Time savings can be particularly important in areas of extreme weather. The house can be made weathertight in a shorter period, limiting exposure to harsh weather both for workers and the interior of the house. When John Engerman built the Greenridge House (see p. 62), it was a particularly cold winter so panelization cut his framing time almost in half.

When panels are built in a factory, weather poses no problem as long as workers can get to work. Material shortage delays are minimized because materials are delivered in quantity.

More Accuracy, Less Waste

Panels are constructed in a controlled environment using sophisticated cutting machines. Walls are straighter and more precisely built.

Panels also result in less waste. Cutoffs and short lengths of wood are more easily recycled in the factory for other projects, and scraps are sometimes burned for heat.

As a shortage of skilled labor and good materials now plague standard construction, panelized construction becomes more attractive. Don O. Carlson, publisher of *Automated Builder* magazine, compares building a house on site to assembling a car in one's driveway, which no one would consider a good idea. For more information about panelization, check out the website- www.nahb.org/panel.

This factory, Sterling Building Systems, is the one in which the Greenridge House was built. An overview can be seen of an entire wall-panel line: the framing station, the area where the walls get sheeting, the area where windows are installed, and the place where housewrap is applied. Photo courtesy Sterling Building Systems

Coastal House

DOUGLAS GOVAN, THE ARCHITECT OF THIS prefabricated home overlooking Maneres Creek in Maryland, set out to make the house Energy Star Certified and to include the latest glass technology, smart house systems, and maintenance-free materials.

The house was designed in a "boomerang" shape to maximize the water and forest views. Govan chose a Shingle Style for the exterior to incorporate multiplaned gables, a pent roof (a small lean-to roof separating floors), a porch, rustic stonework foundation, and casement windows in twos and threes.

Fiber cement shingles were chosen for the siding, and architectural-grade asphalt shingles for the roofing; both are durable, low maintenance, and have long warranties. Faux stone, which is less expensive and easier to install than natural stone, faces the lower portion of the house.

Gas fireplaces in the living and family rooms are not only attractive additions to the house but also supplement the heating system. In case of a blackout, the fireplaces can be used to help maintain the temperature inside the house.

Manufacturer
Empyrean
International, LLC

Project Manager
Andy Grott

Architect
Douglas Govan AIA,
Empyrean
International, LLC

Builder
Lauer Construction
Co., Inc.

Location
Annapolis, MD

Photography
D. Randolph Foulds,
D. Randolph Foulds
Photography,
except where noted

The design of the house takes maximum advantage of the views, giving all common areas at least two exposures. Photo at left by Andy Grott/Empyrean

The flexible track lighting fixture, although not Energy Star rated, is a contemporary addition to the room. The track is narrower than traditional models and can be hand-bent to offer more lighting design options.

The fireplace in the living room is a direct-vent unit, which doesn't require a chimney.

With increasing energy costs, meeting Energy Star requirements seemed logical. In addition to designing the heating and cooling system to be highly efficient, Govan worked with a local lighting designer, Susan Arnold, to design a lighting plan in which at least 50 percent of the fixtures in the main living areas and 25 percent of the fixtures in the bedrooms are Energy Star rated.

Prefabrication Process

All parts of the house were prefabricated in Empyrean International's facility in Acton, Massachusetts, where they built the post-and-beam frame, the panelized open-wall sections with windows and doors, and preassembled stair and rail systems. They also supplied the kitchen and bathroom cabinets.

Lauer Construction prepared the foundation. When the parts were delivered, Lauer erected all of the components and completed the on-site work including electrical and plumbing hook-ups, heating and air-conditioning, an automated lighting system, security and audio systems, and drywall and appliances.

The staircase and railing were preassembled in the Empyrean facility. The window seat is a cozy place to sit on the landing between floors.

First Floor

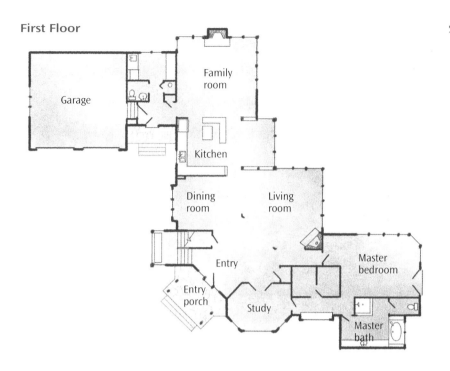

Garage

Family room

Kitchen

Dining room

Living room

Entry

Entry porch

Study

Master bedroom

Master bath

Second Floor

Storage

Exercise room

Home office

Recreation room

Bedroom

Bedroom

Bath

High-Tech Windows

A typical feature of Empyrean houses is a generous use of glass. The sunroom, which surrounds the breakfast room, incorporates passive solar energy. The large windows and walls of glass in the living room and family room are supported by the timber frame. The areas of glass open the house to the forest and water views. All windows have a low-e coating and argon fill.

Smart glass was used in some windows, which change from opaque to clear with the flip of a switch. Smart glass was installed in the front door sidelights for privacy but can be made clear to let in more light. The same glass was installed in the master bathroom next to the spa bathtub so that the window can be made opaque for privacy.

Using privacy glass made it possible to put a low window right next to the bathtub without sacrificing privacy or having window treatments that clutter an otherwise clean look. High windows allow light to stream in throughout the day, and the glass in the low window can be made clear for even more light.

Energy Star Rating

Energy Star is the government-backed symbol for energy efficiency. It identifies new homes and more than 40 types of products that meet strict energy-efficiency guidelines.

To earn the Energy Star, a home must be verified by an independent third party, such as an accredited home energy rater, and deemed to be at least 15 percent more energy efficient than a home built to the 2003 International Energy Conservation Code (IECC). This level of efficiency can be achieved through a variety of technologies and building practices, including the use of high-efficiency heating and cooling systems, air sealing, and high-performance windows. Having an Energy Star-rated house can significantly reduce utility bills, create a more comfortable environment, increase the resale value of the house, and lower ownership costs. In addition, special energy-efficient mortgages are available, along with incentives offered by some utility companies.

Eco-Friendly Flooring

Most of the common areas have bamboo flooring, not only for its sustainability but also for its natural, attractive look and durability. Composite decking, which includes byproducts of wood, was chosen for the two outside decks for its natural appearance and low maintenance.

This house is a good example of the systems and products available today that help preserve natural resources and offer attractive alternatives to more wasteful building practices. It showcases many innovations that will likely become commonplace in the future.

One of the alluring features of this house is the open floor plan with soaring ceilings and walls of windows.

The kitchen is open to the rest of the main floor, which encourages a casual lifestyle.

Because the dining area is open to the living room, tables can be expanded from one room to the other during large gatherings.

The open floor plan was possible because of the strength of the timber-frame construction. The bamboo floor used throughout the first level visually ties several rooms together.

Greenridge House

THE OWNERS OF THIS SHINGLE STYLE

(see the sidebar on p. 67) house wanted a place on Wisconsin's Lake Geneva where they could be close to friends, moor their boat, and entertain their extended family. Fortunately they met builder John Engerman, who owned a spectacular piece of property that perfectly suited their needs.

Challenges remained, however. Local zoning restrictions required 30-ft. side-yard setbacks on this one-acre lot, which is only 60 ft. wide. That left only 30 ft. of building space. The challenge for architect Jason Bernard was designing a 7,100-sq.-ft. prefabricated house that did not exceed the height and width of a house that Engerman had just torn down on the property.

On top of those obstacles, the owners wanted lots of water views, including a view from the front door. Bernard also wanted the house to have entrances from the front, the street, and the lake. Given the room available for building, the house posed quite a design challenge.

Manufacturer
Sterling Building Systems

Builder
Engerman Contracting, Inc.

Architectural Company
Jason Bernard Architect

Location
Lake Geneva, WI

Square Footage
7,100 sq. ft.

Photography
Courtesy Vetter Windows & Doors except where noted

The house has an abundance of windows that take advantage of the beautiful view of Lake Geneva from most of the rooms. The windows also give the house an open and airy feel (above). The panel with the French doors is lifted into place with the crane (left). Photo at left courtesy Sterling Building Systems

Knotty cherry wood cabinets lend a more casual feel to this vacation home kitchen with commercial-grade appliances.

The house was designed with an abundance of custom-shaped windows to take advantage of views and to keep the house bathed in natural light. In the double-height great room, four casement windows were topped with four transoms and then four fixed windows, creating a wall of windows to frame the view. That much glass would ordinarily pose a challenge to maintaining comfortable temperatures. Thanks to state-of-the-art window technology, the double-pane glass with argon keeps the house warm even when freezing breezes blow off the lake. And the shingle siding is nearly impervious to the moisture that accompanies a waterside site.

Because of space limitations, the owners built up rather than out, which resulted in a four-story house. The lower level includes a wet bar,

The bed faces an expanse of windows so the owners can watch the sun rise over the lake each morning. Glass doors open up onto balconies on either side of the room.

Large windows looking out on the lake are the focal point of the living room.

This Wisconsin lake house is distinguished by its classic shingle-style details, including flared upper walls that send rainwater away from the house, tapered columns, and the interesting visual interplay of gables facing the street.

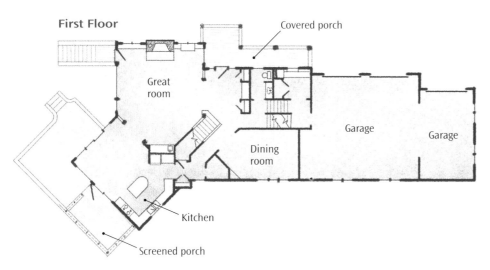

First Floor

Covered porch

Great room

Garage

Garage

Dining room

Kitchen

Screened porch

Second Floor

Great room below

Bedroom

Bonus room

Master bedroom

Bedroom

Master bath

Exterior deck

billiards room, and wine cellar, while the fourth floor features a lookout for enjoying views of the lake. The second floor includes the common areas; bedrooms are on the third floor.

One reason Engerman chose to build the house using a prefabricated panelized system was the –30°F wind chills that can accompany Wisconsin winters. And the heavily insulated system shortened the time it would have taken to frame the house from several months to 3½ weeks. With the success of this Lake Geneva house, Engerman now builds about 80 percent of his houses using panelized construction because it is easier, faster, and more efficient. It also generates much less waste for the landfill.

Shingle Style

What is today called Shingle Style originated in New England coastal towns. It evolved with an emphasis on texture, site sensitivity, and open space. The term Shingle Style was first coined by Vincent J. Scully Jr., a Yale University professor who traced the history of the style in his book, *The Shingle Style,* published in 1955.

The Greenridge House has the typical characteristics of the style, with irregular steeply pitched and multiplaned gables, porches with posts made of stone, rustic stonework foundations, decorative wood structural elements, a pent roof, white painted window trim, and whimsical detailing.

Even from the entrance of the house there is a view of the lake.

Pfaff House

KATHERINE PFAFF LOVES SAN FRANCISCO BAY so much that she built a house on it. Literally. Designed by architect David Marlatt, the house is partly on land, but most of it rests on a steel platform supported by 75-ft.-long concrete piers driven into the bay. The frame is topped with a pressure-treated wood platform that's covered by a layer of insulation and a concrete subfloor, which was expensive but critical.

Constructing a Panelized House

Katherine needed to build the house quickly because of a 12-month construction loan deadline, so she decided to build a panelized house for speed. After considerable research, she chose the Canadian company Nelson Homes to build the house because over 50 years they'd built more than 30,000 homes. Also, the positive exchange rate at the time helped offset the additional shipping cost.

Although some panel companies only sell panels, Nelson sells entire house packages. Katherine selected a standard package with vinyl windows because of the harsh marine environment and

Manufacturer
Nelson Homes

Architect
David Marlatt, AIA,
DNM Architecture

Location
Point Richmond, CA

Square Footage
3,600 sq. ft.

Photography
courtesy Cesar
Rubio Photography
except where noted.

The garages are split and pivoted 45 degrees to reduce their impact on the street while providing easier access from the road. By turning the garages, a sort of courtyard is created and the main entry to the house is placed near the middle of the site (above). The panels being erected on the steel platform went up much more quickly than the base below (left). Photo at left by David Marlatt, AIA

Friends tell Katherine that being in her house is like being on an ocean liner surrounded by water. The house is built on 75-ft. concrete piers and a galvanized-steel subplatform over the San Francisco Bay.

The panels arrived numbered to make it easier to erect them on site. Photo by David Marlatt, AIA

minimal maintenance, but she upgraded to argon-filled glass for added insulation. She also selected fixed transom windows above the steel-clad exterior doors for plenty of light.

As piles were being driven and the steel erected for the foundation, Nelson was prefabricating. The parts arrived on two trucks, and the shell was assembled in two weeks. Although the house was completed in eight months, it took six months to get the permit.

There were many challenges. The local design review committee had to approve every aspect, from engineering and design to exterior railings, landscaping, and light fixtures. "A lot of the challenges were just making the house durable for a marine environment," she said. "We had brass hinges on some of the doors and within a year they were completely corroded; we had to take them all off and replace them with stainless steel." For siding, she chose Hardiplank®, a fiber-cement material, and acrylic stucco for rounded areas and the tower for their durability in harsh environments.

The house was built with plans for the eventual installation of solar panels. The roof was designed to take optimal advantage of the sun, and wiring was installed for the future solar panels. The flat portion of the roof over the bedroom wing was designed for a future third-floor loft.

The Look and Feel of the House

Katherine wanted an open floor plan for the common areas but wanted to make some areas more private. Marlatt designed a pocket door to close off the media room and created an alcove off the kitchen to hide dirty dishes when guests were present. With these small accommodations, Katherine was able to control which spaces were open and which were private.

Although the common areas were designed to be open, Marlatt created a hidden alcove in the kitchen and pocket doors in the media area so private spaces could be created when needed.

This deck on the second floor is used for entertaining and has a sink and barbecue. Because of its location, it is blocked from the strong winds. Katherine was anxious to have a garden, so Marlatt designed an 18-ft. area on the deck for soil and had it reinforced, waterproofing was used for the ceiling area below it. The economical and attractive railing was built on site out of 4x4 posts with stainless-steel cables stretched between them.

The maple flooring is a cool contrast to the warm Brazilian cherry wood used on the stair treads. The circular staircase was found on the Internet, and the aluminum tube railing, found in a local salvage yard, was fabricated by a metalworker.

Like all of the bedrooms in the house, there is a deck off the master bedroom for private sunning. The doors have unmovable transom windows above to let the light stream in.

First Floor

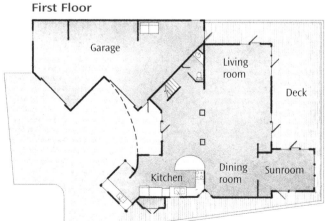

Second Floor

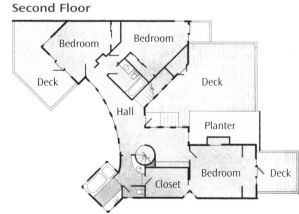

Every bedroom in the house has a private deck. A larger deck on the second floor includes a sink, barbecue, large table, and garden. This deck is sheltered from the wind, which can be strong on the windward sides of the house.

Because Katherine always enjoyed the comfort of radiant heat, she installed the system in her new house. She first balked at the cost, but now says there's no other type of heating for living on water. Her system provides heat to the first floor and master bathroom; the rest of the house is heated by decorative English radiators.

A variety of natural flooring was used. Solid maple floors cover most of the common areas, stair treads are of Brazilian cherry, and Spanish cork flooring is soft underfoot in the kitchen. Square support columns were covered with the circular tubing used for pouring concrete piers, and Honduran mahogany veneer covers the tubes for a warm and natural look.

Wanting the kitchen to be functional and stylish, Katherine used a sink on legs and an oven on wheels to make them look more like furniture. The gas hood was also chosen for its sculptural look.

Katherine found the 1950s vintage Italian light fixture in a local antique store.

Stuctural Insulated Panels

Max Mehlburger, the owner of one of the houses in this book, "can't imagine why everyone doesn't build with structural insulated panels." His sentiment is echoed by many homeowners who have built with SIPs, which account for about 1 percent of houses built today.

Still unfamiliar, SIPs are precut panels used as wall, floor, or roof components. They consist of outer panels, bonded to an insulating foam core. The panels are usually oriented-strand board (OSB), a product similar to plywood.

Little Rock, AR | 6,000 sq. ft.

p 78

East Hampton, NY | 2,400 sq. ft.

p 84

Other options include various types of metal, plywood, cement board, and drywall (for the interior).

The insulating core is typically expanded polystyrene (EPS), polyurethane, polyisocyanurate, or extruded polystyrene (XPS), which is similar in composition to a foam cup.

SIPs can vary in their material composition, method of attachment, and overall thickness. They are usually precut in the factory and numbered to simplify installation by framing crews. They are connected in a variety of joining mechanisms called splines, which are strips of wood or 2x4s that slide into channels cut into the edges of each panel and lock them together. SIPs can be ordered with window and door openings already cut, or the openings can be cut on site.

Electrical chases can be preformed in the factory or cut on site. A new alternative to cutting chases in the insulation is the use of baseboard wiring systems. They make houses more energy efficient because they don't require removal of insulation. Also, changes in the house's electrical system can be easily made.

Because SIP construction creates such a tight envelope, there is an increased need for controlled ventilation, or the exchange of stale indoor air for fresh air. This is usually fixed with an air-to-air heat exchanger or heat-recovery ventilator (HRV). These exchange outside air with interior air, while also transferring heat or cool to the incoming air.

The History of SIPs

During World War I, the U.S. Department of Agriculture's Forest Products Laboratory in Madison, Wisconsin, developed a panel for airplanes. The outer layer was aluminum and the inner layer a honeycomb material for strength. In 1935 they built a series of experimental houses in Los Angeles using SIPs.

Structural insulated panels are commonly used as infill for houses built with timber frames as an energy-efficient and time-saving method of construction. The panels, like the frame, can be prefabricated and erected on site. Photo courtesy Riverbend Timber Framing. Photo by Roger Wade Studios, Inc.

In the 1930s, architect Frank Lloyd Wright also used a sandwich-panel technology in his Usonian houses. The concept was taken further in 1952, when Alden P. Dow, an architectural student of Wright and the brother of the Dow Chemical Company founder, began developing panels sandwiching Dow's Styrofoam™ insulation between plywood panels. Dow built houses in Midland, Michigan, using his newly developed panels.

It has taken years for architects to see the potential of SIPS, for builders to feel comfortable using them, for local building officers to approve their use, and for homeowners to see their potential for energy efficiency and faster construction. Building-industry testing has led to the acceptance of SIPs by most codes.

Using SIPs

SIPs are commonly and increasingly used to enclose timber- or steel-framed structures. They can also be used as the main structural element of the house. Because there are no gaps in a panel's insulation (as there are in stick construction), the panels form a continuous barrier to the elements.

The advantages of panels abound. They can be assembled faster than standard framing. And they save energy. Tests show that SIP-constructed houses are tight and energy efficient. The foam insulation provides higher R-value per inch than fiberglass and creates a continuous envelope around the house. Smaller heating and cooling units are therefore required, and the use of fossil fuel is reduced.

SIPs form the outer walls of the house and can be constructed in a variety of sizes for homes of any style. Once the siding is installed, it is impossible to differentiate a SIPs house from a conventional one.

For further information about SIP construction, go to www.sips.org and www.sipweb.com.

SIPs were used as the structural element in the construction of this house. Panels can be used for any style house and are indistinguishable from traditional on-site construction. Photo courtesy Insulspan, Inc.

Villa Kaki

ITALIANS TEND TO BUILD THEIR VILLAS
of stone, brick, and stucco. Max and Kaki Mehlburger built their
Italian villa of structural insulated panels.

On their many trips to Italy over the years, the Mehlburgers
photographed countless architectural details–downspouts, chimneys,
shutters, roofs, stairs and railings, doors, windows, balconies, all that
caught their eye. So when the time came to sit down with architect
John Jarrard to design their own Italian villa, these photos became
the basis of the design process.

Choosing Structural Insulated Panels

When another architect suggested they
build their house with prefabricated
SIPs, the Mehlburgers researched the
idea and came to the same conclusion.
Otherwise, to meet their local building
code requirements of R-18 walls would
mean compressing R-19 fiberglass batt
insulation into 2x6 stud walls. Yet SIPs
walls of about the same thickness would
provide an R-value of 46— even before
drywall and stucco were added.

Architect
John D. Jarrard

Manufacturer
Fischer SIPS

Builder
Hydco, Inc.

Interior Designer
Kaki Hockersmith
Interiors

Location
Little Rock, AR

Photography
Courtesy Kaki & Max
Mehlburger

The Villa Kaki under construction with the structural insulated panels recently installed (left). This is the same view of the Italian-style villa after its completion (above). The Mehlburgers wanted the house to look like it had been there for ages; this look was enhanced with the warm ochre-color stucco, the Italian traditional trim and roof, and the vines that grow over its outer walls. The design and proportion of the windows in the front court-yard were duplicated from authentic traditional villas in Italy.

When neighbors saw the house being built with solid SIP panels, a rumor spread that it wasn't going to have any windows (top).

The courtyard after the windows were installed (bottom).

Groin ceilings give this hallway the look of having been there for ages.

Besides lowering energy bills, making the house more comfortable, and maintaining interior temperatures more evenly, SIPs also make the house very quiet. Cars going by on the street and airplanes flying overhead are barely a whisper.

Ordinarily, blueprints specify where window and door openings will be cut out. However, delays in the plans, including decisions over the size and number of windows, meant that the panels were ordered whole and the window and door openings cut on site. Erection of the large panels started rumors in the neighborhood that the house would have no windows.

In the Italian Style

The Mehlburgers' large home in the Arkansas capital incorporates many of the architectural details, interior design choices, and materials they admire in old Italian villas. The ceiling in the gallery is a groin vault; all over the house are integrated Italianate niches, pilasters, and extensive moldings; and a local painter created faux finishes throughout, including the wood baseboards in the gallery, which have a faux marble finish to match the floors.

The walls of the wine cellar were faux painted to give them a weathered ancient look. In addition to using the space for storing their extensive collection of wines, the Mehlburgers sometimes entertain there as well.

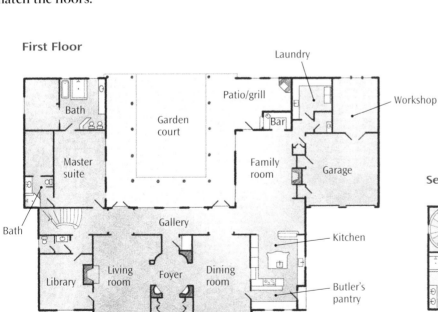

First Floor

Laundry · Patio/grill · Bar · Workshop · Garden court · Bath · Master suite · Bath · Family room · Garage · Gallery · Kitchen · Library · Living room · Foyer · Dining room · Butler's pantry

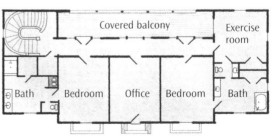

Second Floor

Bath · Bedroom · Office · Bedroom · Bath · Covered balcony · Exercise room

The numerous arches, niches, and moldings are typical of those seen on villas in Italy.

The Mehlburgers put equal effort into exterior details. Kaki found just the right shade of yellow to give the house the look of old Italy; Max added a sundial on the wall over the loggia after admiring a similar one north of Venice.

For the roof, they chose authentic curved clay tiles that are typical in Tuscan design. They also duplicated Italian gutters and downspouts, which have special brackets that secure the downspouts. Max purchased the brackets from Italy, along with downspouts from Michigan, miscellaneous fittings from California, and copper elbows from Germany.

Outdoor Living

The house wraps around a courtyard that was designed for entertaining. On one side of the courtyard they built a large outdoor kitchen. The Mehlburgers used the outdoor kitchen and the pergola in the lower portion of the garden when hosting their daughter's wedding. A long rectangular pond filled with fish that were a gift from a friend sits in the center of the courtyard, and the water flows into a fountain below.

Max ordered the parts for the sundial over the Internet and duplicated the look of those he had seen in Italy. It is functional and "quite accurate," Max says.

Great attention was paid to the courtyard design, which is used extensively for entertaining. The Mehlburgers' daughter was married under the rear pergola.

Chaleff House

BILL CHALEFF AND HIS PARTNER, PAUL ROGERS, were pioneers of environmentally sensitive design. They started their architecture firm in 1987, before the practice of building green or sustainable was popular—or even very well known. Since then, they have built more than 200 energy-efficient houses that utilize passive solar design (placing windows and dense thermal mass, such as a stone floor, to bring in the sun's heat and store it) and active solar design (using solar panels and other technologies to harness the sun's rays).

When Chaleff's own house burned down several years ago, he built a new house that was not only energy efficient but also would utilize as many building materials as possible that were either 100 percent or mostly recycled. Chaleff decided to use SIPs as the main structure of his house. Because he designed the house when SIPs were fairly new, it took almost six years to get approval from his local building department to begin construction. Today, SIPs are readily accepted by building departments.

Architect
Bill Chaleff, Chaleff and Rogers, Architects

Builder
Germano Contracting

Location
East Hampton, NY

Square Footage
2,400 sq. ft.

Photography
Phillip Jensen-Carter except were noted

84

Chaleff designed his own house, as he does for those of most of his clients, using the most sustainable materials and energy-efficient practices available.

Photo left courtesy of Bill Chaleff.

Photovoltaic Solar Panels

Photovoltaic (PV) cells can be assembled into modular panels or fastened directly to special shingles. The panels are grouped into arrays placed over ordinary roofing or can be mounted on the ground. The special solar shingles are used as the actual roofing. When the panels or shingles are exposed to sunlight, small amounts of electricity are released. The current from the solar collector is converted from variable-voltage DC to 120 volts AC. Excess electricity is sent back into the power grid.

Some electric companies share in the cost of installation of PV systems, and some municipalities offer tax rebates or reductions for the use of solar systems. Once installed, PV systems require minimal maintenance and can save the homeowner a substantial amount of money by reducing electric bills.

For further information about solar energy, check the websites of the Energy Efficiency and Renewable Energy Clearinghouse (EREC) at www.eere.energy.gov, and the Solar Energy Industries Association (SEIA) at www.seia.org.

The beauty of the structure is incorporated into the design.

Building with SIPs, Parallel-Strand Lumber, and Steel

Because SIPs have excellent insulating properties, air infiltration resistance, structural integrity, and recyclability, they were a perfect match for Chaleff's environmental sensitivities.

Chaleff chose an engineered product for the beams and trusses called parallel-strand lumber (PSL), which is made by gluing together strips of Douglas fir. PSL is stronger and stiffer than ordinary timber and is less likely to shrink, warp, bow, or split. Chaleff chose a PSL that is manufactured without toxic formaldehyde resins, which can cause problems for some people. Composite steel and PSL trusses run the length of the main space and serve as a design element.

The floor joists and wall studs are made of light-gauge steel, which is less expensive than wood and won't warp, shrink, or expand.

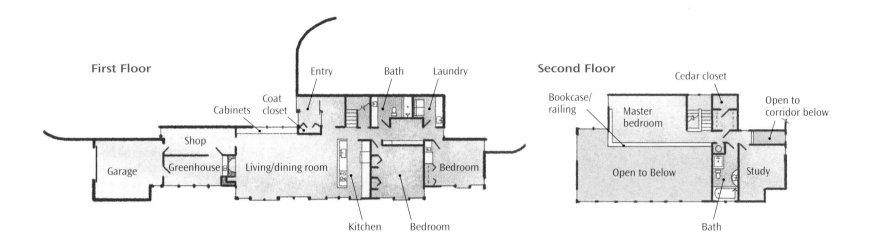

First Floor

Entry · Bath · Laundry · Coat closet · Cabinets · Shop · Garage · Greenhouse · Living/dining room · Kitchen · Bedroom · Bedroom

Second Floor

Cedar closet · Bookcase/railing · Master bedroom · Open to corridor below · Open to Below · Study · Bath

Using Recycled and Composite Materials

"I do not want to be part of the problem; I want to be part of the solution," Chaleff says. Acting on that belief, he uses predominantly recycled building materials. For example, asphalt-impregnated cellulose, which has a high-recycled content, went on the roof.

A fiber-cement siding (Hardiplank) was chosen for the exterior siding. Concrete is highly renewable, making it an ecologically friendly building material. The wood fiber is obtained from fast-growing trees specially farmed for that purpose.

Harnessing the Sun

Many passive solar engineering principles are integrated into the design. Chaleff made the southern facade predominantly glass, so the floor soaks up heat from the sun and releases it during the night. All the glass of the house is double paned with a low-e coating and argon gas filler between the panes to minimize loss of heat.

The house has an open feel with the bedroom overlooking the great room below.

Two sets of solar panels on the rear roof provide much of the energy required for running the house. The windows on the rear of the house were positioned to take the best possible advantage of the sun for the daylight hours.

Two photovoltaic solar panels on the roof reduce electric bills. The system actually runs the electrical meter backwards when producing more electricity than the load requires at the time, which is called "net metering." Chaleff claims his energy bill is one-half of what it would be without the panels. To encourage the use of solar energy, his local power company paid for three-quarters of the cost of the photovoltaic installation.

Smart Home Systems

Chaleff installed an in-floor heating system that works like a hydronic radiant heating system but uses heated air instead of water to deliver heat. In addition to the radiant heating, there also is an air handler for heating and cooling the house powered by a hot water coil from a boiler and a high-efficiency air-conditioning system.

This house is a beautiful example of a highly efficient, comfortable house that uses minimal energy and doesn't negatively impact the environment. Chaleff used the same techniques on most of the houses he designs in the area—saving energy and using natural resources.

The furnishings of the house are simple and functional, consistent with the architectural design.

Artwork is used to add color to the generally neutral tones used for the structure.

Timber frame

p 96
Lakeville, MA | 2,455 sq. ft.

p 102
Sawyer, MI | 2,700 sq. ft.

The soaring ceilings, rich wood, and the secure feeling that comes from seeing the structure of the house all around you: People who live in a timber frame home wouldn't live anywhere else.

In a method that goes far back into history, timber frame construction uses heavy vertical posts and horizontal beams that are held together by mortise-and-tenon joints and pegs. Post-and-beam construction utilizes metal connectors instead of wood joinery and is held in place with wooden pegs. The finished house can be a clapboard-sided cottage or a contemporary design.

Johns Island, SC | 5,000 sq. ft.   p **110**

Bainbridge, WA | 2,580 sq. ft.   p **116**

Innsbrook, MO | 3,250 sq. ft.   p **128**

Big Sky, MT | 5,000 sq. ft.   p **122**

This is one of the beautiful mortise-and-tenon connections that can be used on timber-frame structures. Photo courtesy Davis Frame Co.

Although some homeowners choose to hide the timber frame, others use elaborate trusses and beams to show off the frame's beauty. The soaring ceilings on some timber-frame homes create an impressive volume of space and a wonderful decorative element. Because the weight of the house is carried by the frame, interior load-bearing walls aren't always necessary, which allows for the large, open spaces.

Although "post and beam" and "timber frame" are often used interchangeably, timber frames are always solid wood, including logs, while post and beam may use engineered wood such as glulams, parallel-strand lumber (PSL), and laminated-veneer lumber (LVL).

Timber framing is the more traditional method in which mortise-and-tenon connections are secured with wood pegs, with no metal connectors or engineered wood. Timber-frame construction is generally more labor intensive, and the workmanship is considered to be an art form.

History

Examples of ancient timber-frame construction can be seen all over the world. In Japan and parts of Europe, the frame is kept visible as an integral part of the design; in other areas, the frame is more commonly hidden. Early colonists brought the art of timber framing to North America, where it was the prevalent form of construction until the early 19th century, when mills began turning out uniform sawn lumber and metal nails began to be mass-produced.

It wasn't until the 1970s when a group of craftsmen in New England revived timber framing that it became fashionable again. Today, timber framing is a growing business, with over 3,000 timber framers in North America.

Some companies employ sophisticated machinery, such as the CNC Hundegger K2 (see the sidebar on p. 106) to cut timbers to length and to cut mortise-and-tenon joinery into the wood. Others prefer hand tools as well as large circular chain saws, routers, and chain mortisers, though some use both methods.

Types of Wood Used

Many modern timber framers use recycled or standing dead timbers. Recycled timbers from dismantled structures such as old mills and warehouses are also used. In addition to being more stable, recycled timbers add character and tell a story from their prior use, complete with nail and bolt holes and staining from metal attachments.

River wood, wood that sank as loggers herded huge rafts of logs down the river, develop interesting hues from contact with minerals in the river bottom mud. Other river wood is found in old pilings and piers that spent years in water. Much new-growth wood comes from managed forests, which prevents cutting old-growth trees. Many of the post-and-

The beauty of the timber frame can be seen before the house is enclosed. The timbers for this house were all reclaimed from a warehouse, resawn, and handcrafted by the timber framer. **Photo courtesy Glenville Timberworks; Photographer, Chris Paskus, C&N Photography**

This is the same house after it was completed with precut stress panels. Board-and-batten siding was painted red to make it look like a traditional barn. **Photo courtesy Glenville Timberworks; Photographer, Chris Paskus, C&N Photography**

The soaring ceiling and the intricate joinery are apparent in this handcrafted Douglas fir timber frame home. Photo courtesy Glenville Timberworks; Photographer, Chris Paskus, C&N Photography

beam houses built today could themselves be recycled into new homes in the future.

Timbers used in their "green" state have a high moisture content, which causes wood to shrink as it dries and the structure to move. This movement must be taken into consideration when designing the frame. Some timbers are mechanically dried or air dried to draw out moisture.

The Building Process

The typical timber framer cuts and labels the parts in a shop and ships them to the site. Some companies dry-fit the frame in their yards and then break them down before shipping. With a skilled crew, all but the elaborate frames can be erected in seven to ten days.

Although the frame forms the structure, some form of exterior infill must be used between posts. Early colonists closed up the house using a mixture of hay and mud over wood lath, which was covered by clapboards. Today more sophisticated methods are available that add stability and energy efficiency.

SIPs have become a popular type of infill. In this chapter, the Craftsman's Lodge, the Queenslander, and the House on the Saltwater Marsh were built with SIPs (see pp. 96, 102, and 110). Panelized sections may also be used to close up timber frames. The Coastal House (see p. 56) and the Hobbit Haven house (see p. 122) were all built using panelized sections. In some cases, conventional stud construction infill is used, such as in the Bainbridge Island House and the Far Horizon Reflection Home (see pp. 116 and 128).

Metal connectors can be seen in the wood joinery, making this house a post-and-beam construction but not a timber frame.
Photo by Roger Wade

Timber frames can be used for only part of a house. A frame may be incorporated into a site-built house or added on with the addition of a great room, for example. Two of the houses in this book, Triple Run and the Gallatin River House (pp. 154 and 168), combine timber-frame and log construction, adding visual diversity and creating a practical use of space.

Craftsman's Lodge

Manufacturer
Davis Frame Co., Inc.

Designer
Steve Petty

Builder
Miller Starbuck
Construction

Interior Designer
Karen Corinha,
Corinha Design

Location
Lakeville, MA

Square Footage
2,455 sq. ft.

Photography
Photos courtesy
Davis Frame Co.,Inc.
Rich Frutchey, Photo-
grapher except where
noted

IAN AND JANET EVANS BEGAN THINKING OF building a house soon after they met at the Smithsonian Astrophysical Observatory in Cambridge, Massachusetts, where they worked. After seeing a magazine advertisement, they became interested in timber-frame houses and spent months researching the ancient construction method by attending shows and manufacturers' seminars, purchasing portfolios from several companies, and reading every available book on the subject.

The Design Process

Steve Petty, an independent representative for Davis Frame Co., worked with them on the design. Petty had a clear idea of what the Evanses wanted: a shingled Craftsman Style house with period details including natural colors and windows with a geometric grille design. They also wanted some rounded windows and a rounded roofline on one side of the house to match the shape of the windows.

The Evanses chose this piece of land because it was heavily wooded and sat at the far end of a quiet street. Once construction began, stone ledge was discovered just a few inches below the surface of the driveway and beneath the footings of the northwest corner of the house. Luckily, the builders were able to pin the footings to the rock and raise the elevation of the basement slab by 6 in. so they didn't have to blast.

The basis of their design was a house they had seen in a magazine. When selecting colors for the exterior, they saw the house again on a stain company's website. They called and got the same color stain for their own house.

The Evanses wanted the master bedroom on the main floor because they thought it was a good idea to prepare for a time when climbing stairs would be difficult. They also wanted an open floor plan, which would make their small house feel larger.

The timber frame for the house was manufactured at Davis's New Hampshire plant. It was cut, dry-fitted, numbered, and packed up along with the uncut SIPs for shipment to Lakeville. Contractor Phil Miller poured the foundation while the frame was being completed and later

erected the frame and installed the panels, interior walls, plumbing, wiring, and flooring.

The Evanses buried a liquid petroleum (LP) gas tank on their property so they could cook on a gas stove and enjoy a gas fireplace. They determined that a gas fireplace would be more practical for them since they don't get home until late in the evening and the ability to start a fire at the flick of a switch seemed most convenient.

The large porch is a great place for the Evanses to relax in the warmer months and enjoy the trees that abound on the property.

The circular casement window extends from the guest room into the adjoining bathroom.

Various parts of the timber frame come together with dramatic effect in this entertainment/office area.

Taking an Active Role

The Evanses took an active role in the construction. Ian worked with his brother-in-law, a licensed electrician, to install the wiring, and he completed some of the built-ins. With the help of family, Ian and Janet spent a chilly November weekend applying 32 gallons of stain to the 26 bundles of shingles. The shingles were hung to dry on racks in the garage. A portable heater sped the process. On Monday morning, the bundles were ready for the builder. This event gave Miller confidence in the Evanses' ability to complete tasks, so he turned other responsibilities over to them including more staining and painting, which expedited construction and saved money.

In 2005, Davis Frame won the Cornerstone Award for design and quality given by The Home Builders and Remodelers Association of New Hampshire (HBRANH) for their work on the Evanses' residence.

First Floor

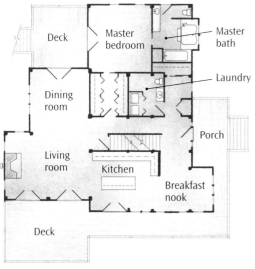

Deck

Master bedroom

Master bath

Laundry

Dining room

Living room

Kitchen

Breakfast nook

Porch

Deck

Second Floor

Open to below

Bedroom

Bedroom

Bath

Many of the small details significantly enhance the look of this house. The geometric grille pattern and grouping of windows add to the Craftsman look of the interior.

A lowered, curved granite snack-bar countertop at the end of the kitchen island invites visitors to enjoy a cup of tea and socialize with the chef while a meal is prepared.

The Queenslander

ON A WINDSWEPT BEACH ON THE EASTERN
shore of Lake Michigan, William Gunnar built a house with views of
gorgeous foliage and bountiful sand dunes. The view didn't come easily.
The home sits at the top of a 90-ft. dune. Gunnar describes building it
as "the equivalent of building on a loaf of French bread." In the end,
he managed to disturb little of the large dune.

The Design Process

On an initial visit to the site, Gunnar noticed a nearby home he thought
attractive and contacted its architect, Howard Holtzman. Gunnar met
with Holtzman, first at the beach where they carved drawings in the
sand and later in Holtzman's studio. Holtzman is credited with making
the association between the "tropi-
cal" Michigan home design Gunnar
was describing and the Australian
Queenslander design.

The northern Australia Queenslander
style is typically a core of central rooms
with a wide porch surrounding it. The
porch offers shade in the summer and
allows the windows to be open when it
rains. Typically, a latticework door adds

Manufacturer
Riverbend Timber
Framing and
Insulspan

Architect
Howard Holtzman
and Associates

Builder
Carlson
Construction

Location
Sawyer, MI

Square Footage
2,700 sq. ft.

Photography
Roger Wade Studios,
courtesy Riverbend
Timber Framing
except where noted

This house looks like it could be somewhere in the tropics, rather than on a sand dune in Michigan (above). The beauty of the frame of the house can be seen before the SIPs were installed (left). Photo at left by Howard Holtzman

to the tropical feeling. Holtzman added several of his own whimsical touches: Metal star cutouts are used on the frame, and columns and fencing are decoratively painted in upbeat, lively colors.

Gunnar had a personal motivation in building a Queenslander-style house. "My great-grandfather, Sir William McMillan, was knighted by Queen Victoria for his efforts in establishing independence for Australia at the turn of the 20th century," Gunnar says. "Although I have never visited Australia, I have heard many stories from my father and his brother. . . . In 1995, my uncle Peter published a biography of my name-sake. I always felt that my ancestors would have been proud knowing I transported a symbol of my Australian heritage to the Michigan shores."

The large great room includes the living and dining areas and opens to the kitchen.

The wide porch is a wonderful place to sip a mint julep while enjoying the foliage and lake views (facing page).

Computer Numerical Control (CNC) Machines

CNC refers to the computer control of machine tools for manufacturing parts in metal, wood, or plastic. These machines take designs and manufacture products without paper ever touching a drafting table. The machines can cut curved and straight pieces faster and more accurately than can be achieved with other tools. The German-made Hundegger K2 is one of the CNC machines commonly used today by timber-frame and log-home manufacturers. The fully automated Hundegger saws all parts including mortise-and-tenon joinery for post-and-beam construction.

Building the Timber Frame

Holtzman recommended timber-frame construction because of its warmth and openness. He had worked with Riverbend Timber Framing and suggested Gunnar contact them. They chose SIPs (manufactured by Riverbend's sister company, Insulspan) to infill the frame because they create a tight and energy-efficient house.

The timber frame and SIPs were prefabricated in Riverbend and Insulspan's Blissfield, Michigan, facility. The SIPs included window and door cutouts. The timber frame was precut with all of the sections prefit. The SIPs and parts of the timber frame were cut with a computer numerical control machine (see sidebar at left), now used in many fabrication facilities.

Steel brackets embedded into the foundation walls made it possible for the porch to be cantilevered around the house.

The precut SIPs are being installed to close up the house. Photos by Howard Holtzman

The framing on the screened enclosure accepts screened or glass panels that can be easily interchanged, depending on the season.

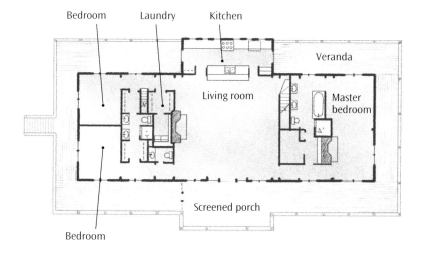

Bedroom   Laundry   Kitchen

Veranda

Living room

Master bedroom

Screened porch

Bedroom

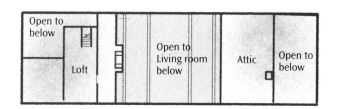

Open to below

Loft

Open to Living room below

Attic

Open to below

The kitchen is open to the great room and equipped with commercial-style appliances, stainless-steel countertops, and custom oak cabinets.

The fireplace in the master bedroom has a glaciated limestone surround, which means that the stone was scored with grooves as it moved across the terrain when it was held in glacial ice.

The children's room was designed with a loft above it that is used as a playroom and an extra bedroom when Gunnar's daughters have sleepovers.

Grey Carlson of Carlson Construction built the foundation, installed the frame and SIPs, and completed the rest of the house. Building on a sand dune required special skills and experience. To build on a dune with frequent spring winds reaching 40 miles per hour demands a level of structural integrity not required in most construction.

The timber frame and SIPs were installed in a week. The balance took almost two years to complete because of additions including a guesthouse and garage. Gunnar says the house could have gone up much quicker if he hadn't made as many changes to the design.

House on the Saltwater Marsh

Architect
Hal Minick, J.A.
Minick International

Manufacturer
Hearthstone, Inc.

Location
Johns Island, SC

Square Footage
5,000 sq. ft.

Photography
Photos courtesy
Hearthstone, Inc.,
by Rich Frutchey

STEVEN AND SANDIE SELENGUT LIVED IN
New Jersey but wanted to retire to someplace warmer and quieter.
They found it on a 10-acre site on Johns Island in South Carolina, an
agricultural area of large plantations that historically grew fruit and
vegetables for nearby Charleston. The site had huge old trees, beautiful
views, and flexible zoning and building code requirements.

When retirement seemed to be too far off, the Selenguts decided
to build a house on the island and move the family and Steve's business there.

Local architect Hal Minick had years of experience designing timber
frames and suggested it to the Selenguts. Minick also recommended
they use Hearthstone, headquartered in nearby Macon, Georgia, to
build the frame.

The Selengut home in New Jersey
was fairly traditional and formal with a
dining room and living room that were
only used twice a year. The new house
would be more informal, open and airy.
The kitchen was designed to open to the
great room so that the cooks could still
visit with guests. The octagonal shape of

An open circular stainless-steel staircase was chosen so that it wouldn't obstruct the water views.

The Selenguts used windows generously to make the house bright and open.

Bainbridge Island House

"Time and trouble will tame an advanced young woman, but an advanced old woman is uncontrollable by any earthly force," Dorothy Sayers wrote. A woman with many interests and great energy, Annette lives a life that's not controlled by challenges and hard work. She takes in abused dogs, tends to her 17 sheep, weaves on her loom, spins her own yarn on a wheel, knits her own blankets, grows her own fruit and flowers, and several years ago, built herself a new home.

Building on a Nature Reserve

When Annette went looking for property, a realtor friend told her about a piece of land that was being sold by a family that had turned most of their land into a reserve and were anxious to preserve the part being sold in any way possible. Annette turned out to be the ideal buyer. She agreed to purchase the property with a conservation easement allowing only 20 percent of the land to be used for buildings.

Manufacturer
Timbercraft Homes

Designer
Judith Landau,
Timbercraft Homes

Builder
Bluefish Fine
Builders

Location
Bainbridge Island,
WA

Square Footage
2,580 sq. ft.

Photography
Craig Wester, Craig
Wester Photography

Annette chose a metal roof because of its looks, the sound it produces when it rains, its fire-resistant quality, and its low maintenance (above). Blueberries, raspberries, kiwis, tomatoes, and an abundance of flowers grow in the yard (left).

Annette added a weaving studio in part of the living room to hold her weaving and knitting equipment.

Standing Seam Roofs

Standing seam roofs are becoming a popular option for residential structures because they are long lasting; resistant to fire, rain, snow, wind, and sun damage; and require minimal maintenance. A variety of metals can be used, from steel to copper.

Panels are either cut and shaped on site or precut in a factory and transported to the home where they are joined to the adjacent panel with double locked standing seams. The interlocking sections are installed vertically from the top of the roof (roof ridge) to the bottom edge of the roof (eaves).

Annette built her house on one side of the 8-acre pasture that abuts the 150-acre Bloedel Reserve, but she was sensitive to maintain her neighbors' views and kept enough open space for her Shetland sheep to graze. Neighbors were used to trotting across the open space that is now her property, and she wanted to minimize the disruption to the area. She now says her house is "an addition to the neighborhood; it doesn't take away from it."

An Inspired Design

Judith and Charles Landau of Timbercraft Homes built Annette's previous home and because a strong bond was formed between them, they were the natural choice to build her new home. Asked where her design ideas came from, Annette says, "I'm not sure where Judith's ideas begin and where mine end." To find inspiration for the new house, Judith suggested that Annette look at some books of the work of Bernard Maybeck, Judith's favorite architect.

Annette had read *Bernard Maybeck: Visionary Architect* by Sally Byrne Woodbridge and liked the interior of a house built with cruck timbers (made by cutting a curved tree lengthwise) and the exterior of another house that Maybeck had built for his daughter. She decided to emulate the timbers of the one house and the concrete look and industrial, small-paned, dark red, true divided light windows of the other. Annette liked Maybeck's Arts and Crafts style but wanted to add touches of Japanese design. For example, with the help of Judith and her builder Gene Knox, she incorporated Japanese tansu-like drawers under the stairs for storage.

Judith was able to take all of Annette's ideas and translate them into a plan with the proper proportion and an attractive, cohesive look. The common areas of the house were built with a timber-frame structure, while the balance was stick framed for economy. The entire frame was cut in Timbercraft's Port Townsend, Washington, yard using sophisticated CNC machinery (see the sidebar on p. 106) and fine woodworking techniques to create the elaborate joinery apparent in the finished home.

It was important to Annette to combine functionality with beautiful design. These tansu-like drawers under the stairs utilize the space and add a unique design element. The cherry-wood cabinet has many small drawers to hold threads, fibers, and the tools Annette regularly uses for spinning wool and weaving.

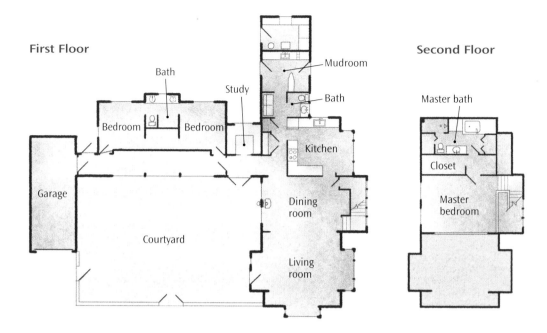

First Floor

Bath

Study

Bedroom   Bedroom

Mudroom

Bath

Master bath

Second Floor

Master bath

Kitchen

Closet

Garage

Dining
room

Master
bedroom

Courtyard

Living
room

**Gene Knox of Bluefish Builders
designed the front door using
19th-century reclaimed timbers.**

All of the joinery was thoroughly checked before it left the manufacturing facility. The frame components were then numbered and transported to the building site on Bainbridge Island, where they were assembled by the same craftsmen who precut the components. The balance of the construction was completed on site by Bluefish Fine Builders. The frame went up in about one week, and the house was completed in about nine months.

A "true" stucco was used on the exterior of the house to imitate the concrete house she liked in the book on Maybeck. The color matched the gatehouse on the adjoining Bloedel Reserve. Neighbors tell Annette that the house looks as though it has been there forever.

Interested in conservation, Annette chose to use as many reclaimed timbers as possible (see the sidebar on p. 146) and to install a hydronic heating system, which uses tubes in the floor to circulate hot water that in turn heats the house. She has the heating system zoned so that she can just heat the area where she lives. The thermal mass of the concrete floors holds in heat, which radiates out at night. Rather than having a wood-burning fireplace, she chose a propane stove. The stove helps to keep the house a comfortable temperature even during a power outage.

The house is an L-shape, one section of which is the guest area for frequent visits from her four children and eight grandchildren. In the

long hallway connecting the guest rooms to the rest of the house, shelves hold a multitude of books. Two guest bedrooms share a linked bathroom and closet. The other section of the house includes the living room, dining room, and kitchen. Annette has a loft above that can be reached via a winding staircase with a ginkgo-leaf cutout pattern on the railing. This design was typically used in fabrics during the Arts and Crafts period.

Annette loves the warm look of wood, even in this master bathroom (top left). The ginko-leaf cutout pattern on the railing carries the Arts and Crafts design through the details (top). The propane stove in the living room supplements the heat in the house, while also adding an attractive element to the room (bottom).

Hobbit Haven

Architect
Edwin Ugorowski
Bitterroot Design
Group

Manufacturer
Bitterroot Timber-
frames, Durfeld Log
& Timber

Builder
Bitterroot Builders,
Inc.

Location
Big Sky, MT

Square Footage
5,000 sq. ft.

Photography
Lonnie Ball &
James Mauri, except
where noted

KIM AND DANA WATKINS BEGAN GOING TO
Montana's Big Sky ski area with their two children to escape the long
lift lines and crowds common to other western slopes. Eventually, they
found more to love there than just skiing: fly fishing in the nearby Gallatin and Yellowstone rivers, hiking, and snowshoeing on mountain trails.

After years of visits, they built themselves a vacation home at
8,000 ft. in Montana's Moonlight Basin. The house is close to the Big
Sky and Moonlight Sky ski areas and has beautiful views. "When you're
looking at the Spanish Peaks from the house, you think this is as close to
heaven as you're ever going to get on earth," Dana says.

Prefabricated Elements

After researching their options, the
Watkinses decided on a timber frame
with posts and beams of massive western
Canadian white cedar logs. Working
with Bitterroot Design Group's architect Edwin Ugorowski, they completed
their design and sent drawings to the
frame fabricator, Durfeld Log & Timber
of Canada.

The massive logs were used to give the warmth of a log cabin, but the panelized infill allowed for additional flexibility with the interior design of the walls (above). The massive logs were delivered with precut and numbered mortise-and-tenon joints to be erected on the prepared foundation (left). **Photo courtesy Durfeld Log & Timber**

When the prefabricated frame arrived at the site, cranes lifted the massive 4,000-lb. logs into place. Other structural details, including panels for the infill, the staircase, and garage doors, were fabricated at Bitterroot's yard.

The house was finished in about a year. Bitterroot's Brett Mauri said it would have taken an additional three months if the homeowners hadn't used prefabricated parts. Not only did prefabrication save the builders time on site, but it also kept them up and running through the winter.

Wide-Open Spaces

A massive array of logs flank the main entrance like ranks of honor guards welcoming guests. The Watkinses named their house Hobbit Haven because of its small front door that's sheltered beneath massive logs. For entertaining, they built a large, comfortable kitchen where family and friends could gather. A fire continuously roars in the stone fireplace that's open to both the kitchen and great room.

The two-way fireplace made of Montana moss rock opens to the kitchen on one side and the living room on the other.

The large, custom front door made from reclaimed timbers has a "speakeasy" that adds to the mythical look of the exterior.

The media room is where family and friends snuggle up to watch a movie and enjoy the warm fire.

The bridge from the clerestory is an easy path to ski slopes or for enjoying a lazy afternoon in the hot tub just beyond.

Photo courtesy Durfeld Log & Timber

All of the rooms were designed for comfort. This children's room includes a window seat for curling up with a great book and an extra bed to accommodate friends.

From the living room windows, skiers can be seen flying down the mountain.

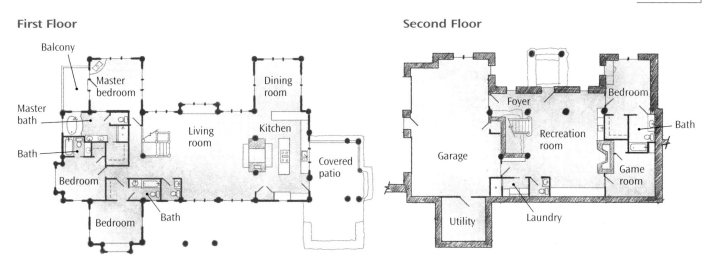

First Floor

Balcony
Master bedroom
Master bath
Bath
Bedroom
Bedroom
Bath
Living room
Dining room
Kitchen
Covered patio

Second Floor

Foyer
Garage
Recreation room
Bedroom
Bath
Game room
Utility
Laundry

The steep site allowed entrances on all levels. The family can exit from the kitchen, through the official front door, or across the bridge on the third level to get quickly to the slopes. When they return, they can choose to enter the bridge on the third floor and relax by the potbelly stove, gazing out the multiple clerestory windows at the mountains beyond.

To create the feeling of a home that has been there for many years, they mixed new materials with old. Kitchen cabinets constructed of reclaimed wood wrap around state-of-the-art appliances. Rustic touches were designed into the house throughout, such as the sliding barn door that separates the master bedroom from the bathroom. The concrete floor was stained the color of moss-covered river rocks. Over-all, the house comes across as eclectic and homey.

Mortise-and-Tenon Joinery

Mortise-and-tenon joinery is one of the most ancient methods of joining wood. Examples from as far back as the Egyptian dynasties have been found. A tenon is a projection cut into one timber that is inserted into a slot, or mortise, on the other timber. If properly done, the joint is as strong as steel. Most tenons are stop tenons, which fit into the tenon and completely disappear. Through tenons go all the way through the connecting member and are often pinned on the other side, frequently in a decorative way.

Mortise-and-tenon joint

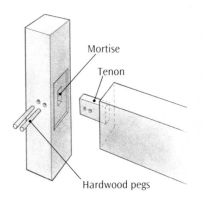

Mortise

Tenon

Hardwood pegs

This cozy master bedroom has magnificent views of the mountains.

Far Horizon Reflection Home

WHO WOULD HAVE IMAGINED THAT YOU could buy a prefabricated home designed by the internationally famous architect who designed Bill Gates' 40,000-sq.-ft. Xanadu house in Seattle's Lake Washington?

James Cutler has a reputation for designing houses that are meticulously created for each site, using the surrounding landscape to determine the layout. Cutler's homes feature large windows that invite the outside world in. He does everything possible to leave trees in place and to fit the house into the land, rather than conforming the land to the house.

When Cutler was approached by Lindal Cedar Homes to create new designs for its portfolio, he first resisted. Most architects design homes for a specific site, and Cutler didn't think it was possible to design prefabricated homes that could be built anywhere. The opportunity to reach more people and the concept of manipulating the prefabricated house forms to fit a particular site won him over.

The design process for Cutler includes walking the land, considering its orientation to the sun, prevailing winds, and topography. With this information,

Architect
James Cutler, Cutler Anderson Architects

Manufacturer
Lindal Cedar Homes

Builder
Innsbrook Custom Homes

Interior Designer
Steve Patton, Frank Patton Interiors Inc.

Location
Innsbrook, MO

Square Footage
3,250 sq. ft.

Photography
Patrick Barta except where noted

128

The massive glass windows allow an abundance of natural light into the house while creating a beautiful vista of the surroundings. It is an attempt by the architect to link the interior space with its exterior environment (above). Photo by Art Grice The house can be seen during construction from across the lake (left).

Photo at left courtesy Cutler Anderson Architects

he can take advantage of the positive aspects of the site, downplay negative ones, and capture the best views. His careful analysis also helps him to avoid disturbing the landscape. For Lindal, he employed the concept of creating houses that have a basic core with wings of rooms that can be attached in a variety of formations. This flexible design allows him to adjust each house to fit the site and the owners' needs.

The master bedroom overlooks the great room, giving it an open look and a beautiful lake view. Photo by Art Grice

The Far Horizon Reflection Home was sited on the property to avoid disturbing the foliage as much as possible while also taking advantage of the lake views.

Movable Parts

The Far Horizon Reflection Home is the first joint venture between Cutler and Lindal Cedar Homes. A prototype, it was built in a vacation community about 45 minutes outside of St. Louis. The core features a cathedral ceiling over the kitchen, dining room, and living room. A loft-like master bedroom overlooks the entry level. One wing contains two bedrooms and a bathroom; the other contains an office and two-car garage.

In future models, the layout of rooms in the wings can change to fit preferences and site requirements, while the main core of the house remains constant. The wings can be shrunk or expanded to include additional bedrooms, guest rooms, baths, or a home office. They can also be rotated to fit the site or to take advantage of views. Cutler describes the wings as "flexible gasket[s]. I can twist them as much as I want to make them fit the particular property." The wings in the Far Horizon Reflection Home were designed to take best advantage of the lake and the sycamore trees that abound on the property. And wood, Cutler's favorite building material, is generously used throughout the house.

The Benefits of Wood-Burning Stoves

With the high cost of energy and a concern for the environment, many people are installing wood-burning stoves in their homes, which trade replenishable firewood for nonreplenishable fossil fuels. Wood-burning stoves warm the house when the lights go out. In rural areas, homeowners often collect firewood from their own land.

Stone was used on the bottom portion of the house for practical reasons, keeping the wood separated from the moist ground and also serving as a natural design element. **Photo by Art Grice**

How They Work Together

When a customer buys one of Cutler's designs from Lindal, the company works with Cutler Anderson Architects to evaluate site plans and photographs, study views, consider the location of plants and significant trees, and learn about any zoning and setback issues. By having customers go through this process, Cutler can feel confident that each house will be sited properly.

First Floor

Second Floor

Like all of Lindal's houses, the Far Horizon Reflection Home was pre-cut in the factory and transported to the site. Cutler's attention to detail is apparent in the exterior facade where stones covering the foundation walls are stacked as natural stones would be, with large ones on the bottom and getting gradually smaller as they reach the top.

A Structure That Connects

In the walkways that connect the core of the house to its two wings, floor-to-ceiling windows further connect the interior and exterior spaces. Cutler designed a special support structure of wood and steel that allows large areas of glass to go nearly to the top of the house and wrap around the sides.

Further blurring the line between indoors and out are two decks built off the rear, between the core and each of the wings. The decks are accessible from the core and the wings, making them feel like continuations of indoor rooms.

The hallways between the core and the wings have extensive windows so that even while walking through the house, the views can be enjoyed. The connections exemplify the architect's attempt to separate the private and public spaces.

Cutler designed a structure that could support the massive windows, taking advantage of the water views. A wood-burning stove was used in the living room to avoid impeding the view.

Cutler designed these connectors, which are functional as well as decorative. He likes the construction elements of the house to show, considering them a part of the beauty of the design.

The kitchen opens to the great room as well as to the porch for ideal casual outdoor dining. Photo by Art Grice

Porches were tucked into both wings of the house, so the outside can be easily accessed from the core or either wing.

Log Construction

p 142

Couer d'Alene, ID | 3,900 sq. ft.

Scandinavian and Eastern European settlers first brought the skill of log building to North America in the 17th century. Settlers moving west carried with them remnants of those skills and began building humble, temporary structures that were generally small and simple in design.

In the late 1900s, wealthy New Yorkers seeking to re-create a romantic past began building log homes in the Adirondack Mountains as weekend and vacation retreats. As the money poured in, the houses became more elaborate and grand.

Northern, IL | 3,200 sq. ft.   p **148**

Big Sky, MT | 12,039 sq. ft.   p **154**

Randleman, NC | 6,340 sq. ft.   p **162**

Gateway, MT | 7,500 sq. ft.   p **168**

The romantic appeal and natural warmth of the wood has lured a growing number of people to build log homes, nearly all of which are prefabricated, shipped, and assembled on site. It is estimated that there are more than half a million log homes in the United States and Canada, most primary residences.

Handcrafted vs. Milled

Although most log homes are built by companies that manufacture log homes with sophisticated machinery, some are still built using hand tools. Handcrafters remove the outer and inner bark layers and alter the profile logs fit tightly. Power tools are used, but notches and profiles are crafted by hand. Logs are scribed in the yard, erected, numbered, trucked to the site, and reassembled. Handcrafted homes are quite labor intensive, which is reflected in their price.

Milled or manufactured log construction is the more common method of building log homes. The logs are mechanically profiled and notched so dimensions are identical. Whereas handcrafted houses are preassembled, milled houses are generally not preassembled, but numbered and shipped with instructions for erecting the house on site.

The Adam Miller Log House was built in 1800 in western Pennsylvania and still stands today in the Somerset County Historical Center.
Photo courtesy the Somerset County Historical Center

The Gallatin River House is a beautiful example of a handcrafted log home that was built with hand tools, some of which are the same as those used for centuries. Photo by Lonnie Ball

Log Home Packages

Most log companies offer a package that includes the shell: log walls, a roof system, doors, windows, porches, and dormers, which accounts for approximately one-third of the cost of a small log home and 15 to 20 percent of the cost of a larger custom log home. The foundation, interior walls, plumbing, wiring, lighting, fixtures, cabinetry, flooring, and other finish work are generally completed by contractors or the homeowner.

Wood Species Options

The wood species usually depends on the house location, what is native to the area, and the type of house. Types vary in diameter and length, color, strength, and structural integrity. Handcrafters generally look for longer logs with less taper and typically use a variety of pine species. Norway or Michigan red pine, readily available near the Maple Island yard, was used for the Crooked Pine Ranch (see p. 148), as was the lodgepole pine, which was used to build the Triple Run house (see p. 154).

Manufacturers of milled houses can work with shorter lengths of wood and often use cedar, hemlock, oak, fir, spruce, or pine. Some companies use an engineered wood product called glue-laminated logs, which are produced by gluing several layers of wood and cutting it into a log shape. Because these do not warp, crack, or twist, they are sometimes preferred for use as structural beams. However, they do require a great deal of labor to produce, so they can be more expensive than natural logs.

Although the moisture content of the wood may vary depending on the type of logs used (such as standing dead wood, green wood, winter-cut wood, seasoned wood, and kiln-dried wood; (see the sidebar at left), log homes must be built to accommodate the shrinkage and settling that naturally occurs with all logs. Logs are generally treated before they are erected and then sealed afterward to repel water and protect against bugs.

Log Home Styles

Log homes are built in a variety of styles and are often dictated by the site. Logs can be cut to a variety of profiles (see the sidebar on p. 152) and with various corner designs (see the sidebar on p. 170) to personalize each house.

Notched or scribed logs fit together tightly to create a weather-proof bond, while others require chinking, which is a synthetic, flexible material troweled between the logs to accommodate the expansion and contraction of the wood, prevent air infiltration, and stop nesting insects. Sometimes chinking is chosen as a decorative element because it resembles early log cabins that were built with a mud and horsehair material layered between the logs.

Nontraditional Options

Although log construction is an old technique, its growth has brought innovations in equipment and methods. For example, a German-made machine called the Hundegger automates the cutting and joinery needed in producing milled log homes. Barna Log Homes used this for part of the Country Dream House (see p. 162).

> Log homes are built in a variety of styles and are often dictated by the site.

Massive logs can be used to build a post-and-beam frame with a variety of infill walls, from whole panelized sections to basic SIPs. These houses have the look of a log cabin with fewer of the maintenance issues associated with stacked logs. Some houses combine post-and-beam and log-stack construction, such as in the Gallatin River House (see p. 168).

Log homes are now available from modular manufacturers, with most of the house built in the factory and delivered as whole boxes or modules (as seen in the Moose Creek Lodge on p. 28) or from panelized companies with whole panelized sections arriving at the site to be erected. For more on log construction, visit the International Log Builders Association web site at www.logassociation.org.

Idaho Chalet

Manufacturer
**Caribou Creek
Log Homes**

Builder
**Campbell &
Campbell, LLC**

**Architectural
Company**
**Cory Trapp, g.d.
Longwell Architects**

Location
Couer d'Alene, ID

Square Footage
3,900 sq. ft.

Photography
**Roger Wade Studio
except where noted**

MERREL AND MARIE OLESEN BOUGHT LAND
and built a vacation home at Idaho's Club at Black Rock because it's
beautiful and it allows them to escape the tourist-filled summers in their
hometown of La Jolla, California. They plan to become summer residents when they retire. And it seemed natural to build a custom, prefabricated log home; after all, it's Idaho. They were a bit nervous, however;
they had never built a home before and were concerned about supervis-
ing the project from so far away. After meeting log home builders Randy
and Mary Campbell, they found people they could trust and allowed the
Campbells to shepherd the process.

g. d. Longwell Architects designed the house and liked the Olesens'
idea of an elegant log home similar to ones they had seen in the Swiss
Alps that have brightly colored windows
and doors.

The architects submitted their design
to log home manufacturer Caribou
Creek, which handcrafted the log
structure in its Bonners Ferry, Idaho,
yard out of standing dead timbers (see
the sidebar on p. 140). The logs were set
on the foundation with a crane. When
the exterior shell was complete, Randy
and his crew finished the balance of the

The roof on the porch, fireplace, and the water feature were added after the house was completed. The Olesens say spending time on their porch is now one of their favorite activities (above). On a misty morning, the precut logs were carefully lifted with a crane and set into place (left). **Photo at left courtesy Campbell & Campbell, LLC**

The red front door and all of the interior doors were custom handcrafted for this house.

The French Lacanche stove helps to carry the red theme through the house.

construction and the landscaping. The house was complete in just less than a year.

The reclaimed wood (see the sidebar on p. 146) Marie chose for the floors was hand-scraped to give them an uneven, handmade texture and finished with a dark, low-gloss oil finish. The kitchen cabinets and all of the interior doors were distressed so that they'd look as though they'd been there for a hundred years. Antique slate tiles were used in the bathrooms, and reclaimed pavers went down in the master shower and tub deck.

After the house was completed, Marie says the deck felt incomplete, so she had Randy add a roof, an outdoor fireplace, and a water feature. Now when she sits on the deck and looks out at the view, she says, "It is magical."

In order to use these 200-year-old pavers on the deck of the bathtub and on the floor of the shower, they had to be sawed to ¼ in.

First Floor

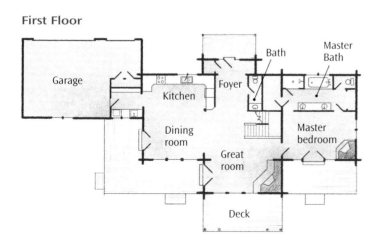

Garage

Kitchen

Foyer

Bath

Master Bath

Dining room

Great room

Master bedroom

Deck

Second Floor

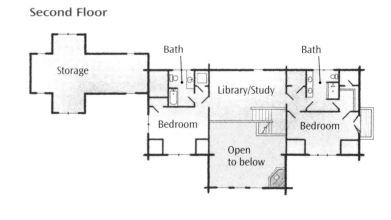

Storage

Bath

Bath

Library/Study

Bedroom

Bedroom

Open to below

Reclaimed Wood

Wood Cuts

Wood can be cut from the log using different angles in relation to the grain.

* Plainsawn

The most common type of cut has more patterning in the wood than the other types because

growth rings are more pronounced. Of all the different cuts, the plainsawn cut provides the widest boards and results in the least amount of waste. It is therefore also the least expensive.

* Quartersawn

The angle of the cut is from 45 to 90 degrees with the surface of the log. It is generally more

expensive, more durable, and, many people think, more attractive than plainsawn. Quartersawn wood resists cupping and twisting and is often recommended for use as a floor over a radiant-heating system.

* Riftsawn

Similar to quartersawn, the annual rings make angles of 30 to 60 degrees to the surface of the

log. It has tighter pores than plainsawn and is the most expensive of all cuts because more wood is wasted sawing it. Along with quartersawn, it is recommended for use over radiant-floor heating because it is also not likely to cup and twist.

* End grain

The growth rings of the wood show because the wood is sliced horizontally across the log. This cut is more durable than plain sawn, but also more expensive.

The staircase was built with the same technology as a timber-frame house using notched connections and dowels. The wood was all wire-brushed to deepen the grain and give it an old world feel.

The chandelier in the living room was handmade by a local craftsman out of naturally shed European fallow deer and elk antlers.

Marie prefers grilling the food when she is doing the cooking, so the outdoor fireplace serves as an excellent place to barbecue and create simple meals.

The dining room is a great place to gather when the Olesens' children and grandchildren come to visit.

Crooked Pine Ranch

Architect
Gordy Hughes

Manufacturer
Maple Island Log
Homes

Builder
Steven Fox, Custom
Log Structures

Interior Designer
Simeone Deary
Group

Location
Northern Illinois

Photography
Roger Wade Studio

WHEN CARLOS AND DEBBIE VISITED Aspen to
accept a Food and Wine Classic award for having one of the best restaurants in North America, they fell in love with the town's log cabins.
Over eight years, they read magazines and attended log house raisings
until they were ready to build their own.

At first they weren't sure how they wanted their log home to be built,
but they knew they wanted the logs to be handcrafted and the house to
have a rustic look. They researched log home construction companies in
their area and decided on Maple Island Log Homes.

Carlos and Debbie met with Maple Island architect Gordy Hughes
several times before settling on a floor plan. Their original intention was
to build a modest 1,500-sq.-ft. second home, but as the project pro-
gressed it became clear that this would become their permanent home.
So they began to increase the size, adding space, including a large wine
cellar to accommodate their collection of fine wines—ending up with an
upscale 3,200-sq.-ft. cabin.

Crooked Pine speaks to the unusual names that camps, cabins, and
ranches traditionally get. There had been a tree farm on the land, and

The homeowners wanted their house to have a rustic look on the exterior, with hand-hewn full logs and chinking.

The second-floor "catwalk" overlooks the great room, adding to the open feeling of the house.

The stone fireplace was built with natural stones from the local northern Illinois area.

some of the trees remain including trees such as blue spruce, Scotch pine, red pine, and fir. For some reason, many of the pines on the site were crooked, hence, "Crooked Pine Ranch." To formalize the name, they had stone columns built with a log across them holding the name placket, as they had seen on ranches out west.

Construction took about a year and a half. While the foundation was poured, Maple Island cut the logs and dry fitted the house in their construction yard. Over three months, crews completed the cutting and assembly, then shipped the house to the site. Maple Island erected the house in three days. The builder, Custom Log Structures, completed the room partitions and finish work.

The stone pillars with a log that spans across suspends a plaque with the name of the house—Crooked Pine Ranch. Inspiration for this structure came from the owners' trips out west.

Log Profiles, Chinking, and Corners

A variety of wood profiles are available for logs, such as the full-round log used on the couple's home. Other options include a Swedish cope, which is round with a groove on the bottom so each log nests into the log below; rectangular logs; beveled rectangular logs; square logs; and D-logs, which have flat tops and bottoms and a curve on one or both sides.

Round logs always require chinking, which is an insulating and waterproofing acrylic material used to fill the cracks or joints between the logs. The flexible acrylic is mixed with sand to mimic the look of traditional chinking. Foam backer rods are placed snugly in the space between each log. These both seal the space and create a surface for the chinking material to adhere to.

All the Bells and Whistles

Different design features and room layouts make this log cabin unique. The master bathroom has many modern touches, such as a vessel sink and a shower without a door. Limestone covers the bathroom floor, which slants toward the drain. The antler chandelier over the claw-foot tub and hanging lantern lights on either side of the rustic wood cabinet let you know you're still in a log cabin.

The kitchen is perhaps the most important room of the house for restaurant owners. While busy schedules mostly keep them out of their own kitchen, Debbie cooks breakfast every morning and dinner on Tuesdays, which is their day off. The couple's chef used to teach cooking classes in their restaurant kitchen but now holds them in the log cabin kitchen. The grand 12-ft. island makes it convenient for 8 to 10 students to attend each class.

First Floor

Covered porch

Open deck

Hot tub

Dining room

Great room

Master bedroom

Screened porch

Entry

Kitchen

Master bath

Second Floor

Bedroom

Open to great room

Bath

Bedroom

Open to entry

The off-white concrete vessel sink, which has the look of an old-fashioned mixing bowl, adds a beautiful contrast to the dark warmth of the logs in the powder room. It sits on a console that was custom made out of reclaimed barn wood.

This gracious kitchen contrasts rustic 100-year-old barn wood cabinets with modern commercial-grade appliances.

Triple Run

Manufacturer
Bitterroot Timber-
frames

Architect
Locati Architects

Project Manager
Andrew
Brechbuhler

Builder
Bitterroot Builders,
Inc.

Interior Design
Michelle Varda
Varda Interiors

Location
Big Sky, MT

Square Footage
12,039 sq. ft.

Photography
© Karl Neumann/
www.karlneumann
photo.com

IT MAY LOOK LIKE A TRADITIONAL, ALBEIT enormous, log cabin, but the Triple Run compound is a largely pre-fabricated, state-of-the-art masterpiece. Nestled in the mountains of Big Sky, Montana at 9,000 ft., Triple Run consists of a multilevel main house, an attached guest apartment, a semiattached guest cabin, and a three-car garage.

The old world charm of a handcrafted log home combines with the latest modern technology. The house is equipped with a smart-home system that provides a variety of lighting configurations, a home theater, commercial-grade kitchen, and a heated lap pool. The roof is a synthetic shingle, which looks like slate but is durable enough to stand up to the heavy Montana snows.

Although uncommon in traditional log cabins, large double-glazed windows that frame the amazing views are found throughout. "The architecture of the house is almost a contemporary interpretation of an age-old traditional building method," Bitterroot Builders' Brett Mauri says. "You would never see this number of windows in a historic example of the architecture that inspired this house."

This gorgeous 4.4-acre compound is situated on a cul-de-sac at 9,000 ft. in the Yellowstone Club in Big Sky, Montana, and consists of a main house, an attached guest apartment, a semiattached guest cabin, and a three-car garage. The separate facilities were designed to accommodate guests and provide them with private space.

The dining table, built by Bitterroot, and the antique chairs that were purchased at an auction provide a comfortable area for the owners and guests to gather for meals.

Recycled Roofing Materials

A variety of recycled roofing materials that resemble cedar shake and slate are available. Although costs are similar to natural materials, synthetics are resistant to hail, sunlight, wind, mold, mildew, fungus, rot, and freeze-thaw cycling conditions. Most have a high fire-resistance rating.

The roofing requires little or no maintenance, and most carry an extensive warranty. The material is light and, in the case of artificial slate, doesn't need the extra structural support that natural slate requires.

Log-Home Construction

Like many of the custom log homes built today, a variety of construction techniques went into Triple Run. The main house is stacked logs. Other areas use log post-and-beam construction, which in the kitchen, family room, and primary staircase is made of salvaged barn timbers.

Each log was hand scribed in Bitterroot's shop using age-old techniques. "When you are using handcrafted logs, there is only one match for every log. They are not interchangeable with any other log in the house, since each was hand scribed to its mate," says Mauri.

The garage and caretaker suite above was conventionally framed, but, like the logs, the frame was measured and cut at Bitterroot and transported to the site. About 80 percent of the house was prefabricated to ensure accuracy, save time, and avoid waste. "This allows us to control on-site labor costs, which are more expensive in a remote location than in a controlled environment," the builder says.

The kitchen is equipped with every amenity including commercial-grade appliances, warming drawer, granite countertops, custom cabinetry, and a huge walk-in pantry.

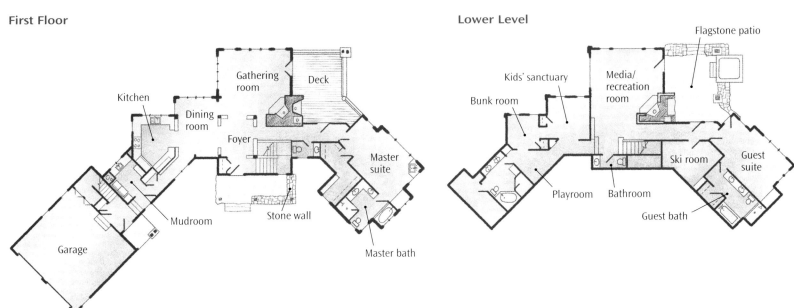

First Floor

Kitchen

Dining room

Gathering room

Deck

Foyer

Master suite

Mudroom

Stone wall

Master bath

Garage

Lower Level

Flagstone patio

Kids' sanctuary

Bunk room

Media/recreation room

Playroom

Bathroom

Ski room

Guest suite

Guest bath

The lower-level family room is part of the guest suite designed to provide privacy for guests in a self-contained area.

The logs used to build Triple Run were standing dead, handcrafted lodgepole pine and spruce. Logs range in diameter from 16 in. to 32 in. A half-moon cutout along the bottom of each log ensures a tight fit.

The homeowners were determined to incorporate into the house "root-base" logs, which have the naturally curving base of the trunk intact. Root-base logs come from trees that have fallen, which makes them fairly rare. They were used in the exterior of the house as well as in the great room and dining room.

Root-base logs have a magical forest look to them as they appear to be growing out of the floor they sit on.

This massive waterfall was a design challenge but it's one of the things that makes this home unique.

The dramatic entry hall has the unique flooring made from slices of logs with multiple layers of resin. The entry door is from ancient China, which the owner purchased at auction. It was fabricated by Bitterroot to open as a 5-ft. door or as a 12-ft. door with the custom door built around it.

Challenges Met

For the main entry, the homeowners purchased two antique Chinese doors. However, the doors didn't function correctly so Locati Architects redesigned the entryway and incorporated the antique doors into the new doors for a unique effect. Using reclaimed oak timbers, Bitterroot built the new doors around the antiques so that both the original 5-ft. doors and the new 12-ft. doors are operable. Inside, visitors step onto the unique entryway flooring, which is made out of round slices of heavily sanded logs finished with more than 30 coats of waterproofing resin, then surrounded by pea gravel. All in all, the feeling is of tiptoeing through a Chinese garden.

The dramatic main entry to the house from the exterior.

The entertainment deck includes a spa, a dramatic fireplace built with Chief Joseph stone, and an outdoor kitchen.

The bronze sink was selected because its trunk shape was consistent with the overall design of the house.

The owners can swim in the current pool in the lower level of the house even in the coldest days of winter.

Country Dream House

Manufacturer
Barna Log Systems,
LLC

Builder
Country Living
Log Homes

Location
Randleman, NC

Square Footage
6,340 sq. ft.

Photography
Roger Wade Studio

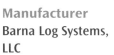

THE SMALL, 200-YEAR-OLD LOG HOME
that Lisa and Eddie Tysinger and their two sons lived in was bursting
at the seams. The time was right to build their own.

Lisa, who works with Eddie and his father, Jock, selling and building log homes as a distributor for Jim Barna Log Home Systems, had
decided that building a model home that they would live in might allow
them to showcase their business and to get that larger place they'd been
needing.

Naturally, the Tysingers chose Barna to fabricate their house. They
had worked with them for years. And Barna used state-of-the-art
machinery to produce its unique homes of kiln-dried logs that were precut in its factory with a double tongue-and-groove profile, making them
strong and watertight.

Barna would cut, assemble, number, and disassemble the home; the
Tysingers' crew would put it together.
Typically, assembly takes 4 to 10 weeks,
depending on size. However, their home
took a year because they were constantly
taking crews off their own house to work
on customers' houses.

Prow windows are commonly used on log homes to let in an abundance of light and to take advantage of the natural habitat surrounding the house.

The massive prow window showers the great room with sunlight, and the efficiency of the windows cuts down on the need for air-conditioning and heating.

Faux stone was used for trim around the exterior of the house for its ease of installation and cost efficiency.

The Tysingers chose a precast insulated foundation system from a company called Superior Walls® (see the sidebar on the facing page). The Tysingers completed all aspects of the construction for their own home, but customers generally have them do the "dry-in" portion of construction, which includes stacking the logs and installing the roof, exterior doors and windows, porches, decks, and interior stud walls. Customers then have the option to hire their own contractor to complete it.

Building a House for Themselves

The Tysingers chose a standard plan from Barna's portfolio and customized it. Lisa wanted the back of the house to be as interesting as the front because both sides are visible from the road. A "prow" window, framed with massive, hand-peeled hemlock half logs, was added to the front. A porch, gabled dormers, and stone accents were added to the rear to make it as beautiful as the front. The screened porch Lisa had always wanted was added along with a wraparound porch for entertaining. Many of their new customers now want them to duplicate the design for their own homes.

It took several years to complete the one-of-a-kind plan. For the logs, they chose a saddle-notched corner design (see the sidebar on p. 170) and 10-in.-round logs with a double tongue and groove, which don't require chinking. Drywall was used for some interior walls, which Lisa painted in earth tones to complement the logs. She used an opal stain for a pickled, whitewashed look on the tongue-and-groove plank walls in the bedroom and bathroom, and a clear stain for the other walls.

Precast Foundation System

Precast technology has been used commercially for years but only in the last decade has it been used for house foundations, which are precast, shipped to the site, and lowered and locked into place with a crane. Some systems include insulation; others do not.

In the Superior Walls system, which the Tysingers used, each concrete panel contains insulating polystyrene and rebar. Precast systems are poured with openings for doors and windows, as well as wiring access and wood or metal furring strips for attaching drywall or paneling.

Installing the precast foundation for a typical house normally takes less than a day. Once in place, the house can be constructed immediately. With an ordinary foundation, this might take as much as two weeks.

For more information, check the website of the National Precast Concrete Association at www.precast.org.

The Tysingers chose natural earth tones for the decor of the master bedroom to complement the warmth of the logs.

The floor-to-ceiling stone fireplace opens to the great room and the dining room on the first floor. There are also openings in the basement below and in one of the bedrooms on the second floor.

The maple cabinets and granite countertops add textural interest and contrast to the abundance of pine.

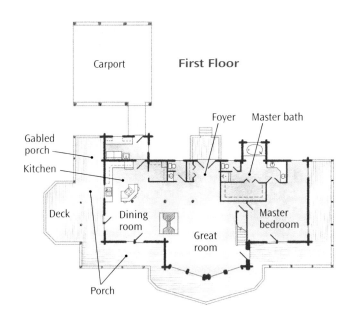

Carport

First Floor

Gabled porch

Kitchen

Foyer

Master bath

Deck

Dining room

Great room

Master bedroom

Porch

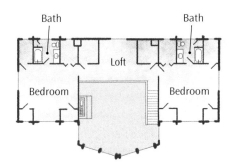

Second Floor

Bath

Bath

Loft

Bedroom

Bedroom

Exterior logs were white pine, but the interior finishes were made from several species. The flooring on the first story is antique gum wood, reclaimed from a 150-year-old tobacco barn. Its interesting color and character make this hard-to-find wood especially unique. The planks are random sizes ranging in width from 3 in. to 11 in. Upstairs, yellow pine flooring was installed.

For heating and cooling, the Tysingers chose an efficient system with four electric heat pumps and two hot water heaters to create four heating zones. Combined with the thermal mass of the logs, the system keeps their house comfortable on cold nights. Ceiling fans push hot air back down into the rooms below. Fans on the porch create a gentle breeze on hot summer days.

The Tysingers liked the look of dry-stacked stone for the great room fireplace and for exterior stone accents. Because natural stone is expensive and stacking very thin stones is labor intensive, they chose cultured stone, which is less expensive, lighter, and easier to install but gives the same random look as real stone.

The Tysingers believe their new home will last for generations, just like their 200-year-old log home has. Lisa's customers have always told her how unique and special they've found the experience of living in a log home to be. And after living in one herself, Lisa understands what they mean.

The Tysingers designed the porch with screened-in areas for warm evenings when the insects are buzzing around and open areas to take advantage of the sunlight.

Gallatin River House

When Serena and Mike Highum

purchased 20 acres overlooking the beautiful Gallatin River, they knew what they wanted: a spacious log home where they and Mike's five children could spend vacations fly fishing, kayaking, rafting, and entertaining. And for ski season, the Big Sky ski resort was only six miles away.

Serena has a background in interior design and spent months sketching how she wanted the rustic but elegant house to look. It would be shaped like a boomerang, with a central "cabin" in the middle and two wings on either side, all facing the river. She and Mike collected pictures of architectural elements in preparation for working with the architect for Bitterroot Builders.

A Combination Approach

Although the original plan called for a house built only with stacked logs, it developed into a hybrid–part log and part post and beam with a panelized infill system. The result is an interesting fusion of three different types of construction.

Architect
Edwin Ugorowski
Bitterroot Design
Group

Manufacturer & Builder
Bitterroot Timber-frames & Bitterroot Builders, Inc.

Location
Gallatin
Gateway, MT

Square Footage
7,500 sq. ft.

Photography
Lonnie Ball and
James Mauri, except
where noted

168

The house is nestled among a variety of evergreens designed to take the best possible advantage of the beautiful views of the Gallatin River (above). The logs were assembled in the Bitterroot yard, then numbered, taken apart, and transported to the home site to be reassembled (left).

Log Home Corner Design

Corner designs can significantly influence the look, cost, and speed of log home construction. Some companies offer just one design, while others offer several. The saddle-notched corner used on Country Dream House, Crooked Pine Ranch, and Gallatin River House is one of the most popular designs.

Other options include interlocking corners, dovetails, butt and pass, and corner posts, the latter of which gives a more formal finish to the house.

Interlocking corners

Dovetail corners

Corner post

Butt-and-pass corners

Saddle-notch corners

The great room is the centerpiece, built using stacked-log construction, as is the left wing, which contains the master suite, an extra bedroom and bathroom, an artist's loft, and a sitting room. The other wing, which includes the kitchen, bunk room, guest suite, and garage, is a massive log post and beam construction.

Like all houses built by Bitterroot, the logs are made from standing dead spruce and pine trees. Both the log-stacking system and the infill panels were built and assembled at Bitterroot. They cut and numbered the parts and transported them to the site. The corner design for the logs is a saddle notch, which is a traditional style most often used in handcrafted log homes. The logs are full rounds and use chinking as a design feature and to create a watertight bond between logs.

The central point of the living room is the large hearth built with natural local stones.

These custom bunk-bed units are an efficient use of space, and the curtains provide privacy for the children.

Bitterroot built a natural climbing wall for the children with rocks sticking out randomly.

Made for Kids and Guests

Because Mike's children spend one month each summer and some of their winter vacations with their dad, the Highums designed the "bunk room," which has four bunk beds for the kids, each with a curtain, a recessed bookshelf, and a small reading light.

The Highums widened the long area between the central core and the guest room and put in a computer desk, built-in game table, and an L-shaped window seat. They call this long area the "bowling alley," and it is a great place for the kids. By rethinking this space, "We don't feel like we have a hall; it's functional," Serena says.

The kitchen walls are plastered, which provides for relief from the dark logs and a better surface for hanging cabinets. The room is painted a cheery buttercup color.

Serena refers to the long upstairs hallway as the "bowling alley," which she wanted wide enough so that it would be usable space.

Bitterroot's architect and masons created a perfect focal point for the massive gathering room: a large masonry fireplace (with a fire that hardly ever goes out when people are in there). "The art of building true masonry fireplaces is being lost to prefabricated fireboxes, which are faster, cheaper, and easier to build," says Bitterroot's Brett Mauri. This particular fireplace was a tour de force of the mason's art.

The house is great for entertaining, which the Highums do a great deal. The sitting area and dining table are in the same big room, which is open to the kitchen so everyone stays together. Serena designed the kitchen so several people can use the kitchen at the same time. When she's not entertaining, Serena likes to spend time in the loft above the

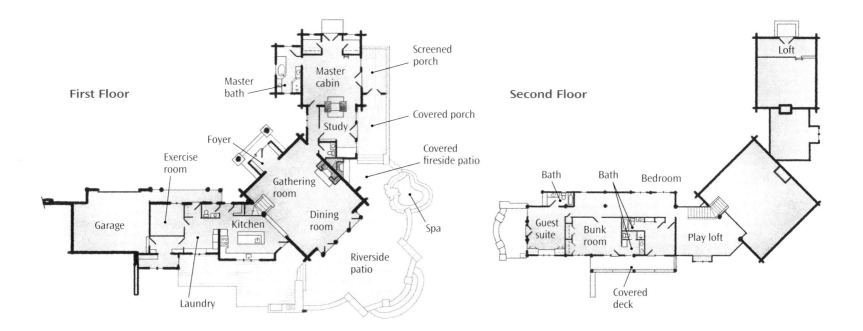

First Floor

Master bath

Master cabin

Screened porch

Study

Covered porch

Foyer

Covered fireside patio

Exercise room

Gathering room

Spa

Kitchen

Dining room

Garage

Riverside patio

Laundry

Second Floor

Loft

Bath

Bath

Bedroom

Guest suite

Bunk room

Play loft

Covered deck

The dining room was designed to be part of the great room for casual family gatherings.

The artist's loft above the master bedroom was designed so Serena could have a private space in which to work. French doors open the space to a balcony that overlooks the river.

The private study connects to the master bedroom which is made from log stock.

master bedroom, which is equipped with a sink and French doors leading out to a balcony. This is her private space.

Because the river views were so important to the Highums, Edwin Ugorowski, one of Bitterroot's architects, put great effort into situating the house. "I don't think the house could have been placed more perfectly than it is," Serena says. "Every window is like a picture frame with a beautiful view of the river." The bunk room and guest suite on the second floor have doors leading to a covered porch. The master suite and great room on the first floor also have doors leading outside.

The expansive rear patio has an outdoor fireplace, a built-in barbecue, a hot tub, and a large table for gathering. And the river is just 30 ft. to 40 ft. down the hill where they had a fire pit built for the most informal type of dining.

The Highums enjoy the beauty of the logs and rustic look of the chinking as well as the contrast of the plaster walls in other areas of the house.

The house was designed so that most of the rooms look out on the beautiful views and open to the exterior space. And the fire pit close to the river is a favorite spot for casual barbecues.

Concrete

Concrete as a building material is as old as the Roman Empire. And it has been used for years in Europe due to the shortage of trees. However, the concrete house is a comparatively new trend in the United States.

The Milton House, built in 1844, was reportedly the first concrete house constructed in the United States. The "grout" was a mixture of burnt lime, stone, gravel, and water. The Milton House still stands in Milton, Wisconsin, and is currently a museum. In the early 1900s, Thomas Edison built inexpensive but cozy concrete houses in Union, New Jersey, many of which

p 182

Prairie Grove, IL | 9,200 sq. ft.

p 188

Henderson, NV | 4,300 sq. ft.

The Milton House, reportedly one of the first concrete structures built in the United States in 1844, is still standing in Milton, Wisconsin, a credit to the durability of concrete.
Photo courtesy the Milton Historical Society

remain standing. Frank Lloyd Wright, an advocate of concrete construction because of its strength and design possibilities, designed the Fallingwater house using slabs of concrete.

Why Concrete?

There are many reasons why people have chosen concrete. The strength of the material makes it practical in areas prone to tornados, hurricanes, and forest fires; concrete houses often survive storms and hurricanes when stick-built houses around them are devastated.

The thermal mass and airtight qualities of concrete can reduce heating and cooling requirements, which often results in significant energy savings. Concrete is resistant to rot, rust, and termites and reduces sound transmission. Upkeep is often minimal.

Because of the strength of the material, some insurance companies offer discounted rates for concrete houses. Concrete is also an excellent choice for people concerned about the environment because it is highly recyclable and requires less energy to create than many other building materials.

Although building with concrete is generally more expensive than building with wood, its energy efficiency and disaster resistance are often considered equalizing factors. In the past, it has been difficult to find builders with the experience to construct concrete houses. This has become less of an issue in the last several years as many companies that produce concrete building systems now offer training to builders. These systems simplify construction by manufacturing parts of the house in a factory.

Two Examples

In this chapter, much of the construction of the two concrete houses was prefabricated. For the precast insulation system used in the Jesse Road House (see p. 188), the walls were poured in the controlled conditions of a precast concrete factory with the help of a computer program that prepared a design for wall panels and assisted in evaluating the structural requirements necessary for each wall.

The walls are cast on a large steel plate with the interior face going down first. After the walls and openings are formed on the table, the reinforcement for the interior wall, the electrical outlets and conduit, and any imbeds are put into place. A 4-in. layer of concrete is then poured onto the table, followed by polystyrene insulation. A nonconductive composite connector that will hold the two layers of concrete together is installed through the foam. The exterior layer of concrete is then poured onto the foam and troweled to a finish. The interior wall finish is so flat and smooth that it only needs to be painted. When the panels are complete, they are shipped to the site and quickly erected with the help of a crane.

In the Smith House (see p. 182), an insulated panel system called Solarcrete™ was used. A prefabricated panel consisting of about 7 in. of expanded polystyrene (EPS) insulation is sandwiched between two

The concrete floors in this house act as a thermal mass, which in cold climates can absorb heat during the day and slowly radiate it at night. In hot climates, the concrete can be a source of coolness.

With this insulated panel system of construction, the expanded polystyrene (EPS) insulation panels, which are sandwiched between two parallel sheets of wire mesh or rebar, are erected first. Next, shotcrete, a form of concrete, is sprayed onto the panels. **Courtesy of Steven Smith**

What is Thermal Mass

Thermal mass is a solid or liquid material that can absorb and store warmth and coolness until needed. High-density materials such as concrete, brick, and stone have the ability to store and release energy back into a living space. Proper placement of these materials in floors, interior walls made of adobe or brick, or a large stone or brick fireplace will increase the amount of thermal mass in the home and make it more energy efficient. During the summer heat is absorbed in the cooler surfaces of the home, which keeps the space comfortable and reduces the need for air conditioning. In winter the same thermal mass materials can store heat from the sun or heaters and release it at night when the room's air temperature falls. This is the concept that makes the stone-tiled breezeway in Sunset's Breezehouse so effective as well as the two concrete houses in this book.

parallel sheets of wire mesh or reinforcing bars and held together with ties. The preengineered panels are then transported to the site and attached to the foundation with steel dowels, which were precast into the foundation.

Spaces are cut out for the windows, doors, and plumbing, and wires are snaked through the foam insulation before the panels are coated with about 3 in. of concrete sprayed onto each side. After the concrete is applied, the surface is troweled to a smooth finish. The result is a wall approximately 12 in. thick.

For both systems, the architects and homeowners had to be diligent about planning to make sure adequate electrical conduits and outlet boxes were installed before the panels were constructed. To prepare

The Difference Between Cement and Concrete

Cement is an adhesive made of clay, shale, iron ore, and limestone that binds stones and sand together to form concrete. Cement usually refers to Portland cement, a generic name for the type of cement that comprises about 10 to 15 percent of the concrete mix.

The prefabricated insulated concrete panels are lifted with a crane and placed on the foundation. The walls for this 4,300-sq.-ft. home were erected in one day. Photo courtesy of The Dow Chemical Company

for future needs, both homeowners chose to include more wiring and outlets than were required.

The concrete portion of the Jesse Road House was erected in a day, while the panels for the Smith House took several months to complete. Timing wasn't the only issue to either of these homeowners in selecting a concrete system. Both owners considered the strength of concrete, its energy efficiency, and its noise-reduction qualities more important factors.

For a broader understanding of concrete, its uses and its properties, try visiting the Portland Cement Association's rich web site at www.cement.org. The PCA has a Google-powered search engine that allows you to find information specific to your needs.

Smith House

Architect
Douglas Farr,
Carol McLaughlin,
Patrick Thornton,
Farr Associates

Manufacturer
National
Solarcrete Inc.

Location
Prairie Grove, IL

Square Footage
9,200 sq. ft.

Photography
Photos courtesy
Farr Associates

TWO AIRLINE PILOTS SET OUT TO BUILD
their dream house. They wanted a peaceful oasis to enjoy their time off
together. They wanted a modern house with high-tech systems.

Steve Smith was primarily concerned with a method of construction
that was sustainable, while his wife, Jackie, wanted the design of the
home's interior to connect with the outdoors.

They considered all the usual methods of construction, but it wasn't
until Steve and architect Douglas Farr visited a house being
built with a concrete system called Solarcrete that the solution became clear.

Unlike some other concrete building materials, this
system involves a sandwich of insulation between layers of
concrete, creating an excellent insulating envelope and providing thermal mass to even out temperature fluctuations.
"Houses in this country are built as disposable commodities
and, environmentally, we didn't think that was the way to
go," Steve says. "We wanted a house that could withstand
the elements for a minimum of a hundred years."

The Smiths spent two years actively involved in planning
their house. Because of the intricacies of the design, the
working drawings were elaborate. The final plan included a
mother-in-law suite, wheelchair accessibility throughout the

The house was designed and positioned on the property to take the best possible advantage of the sun in heating the house (above). The insulation panels were lowered into place with a crane and then connected to the foundation (left).

Garage

Mudroom — Laundry

Sleeping porch

Lanai

Formal dining room

Parlor

Covered entry

Master bath

Great room

Office

Master bedroom

Kitchen

Greenhouse

Roof deck

Bath

Bath

Bedroom

Bedroom

Bedroom

Airfloor System

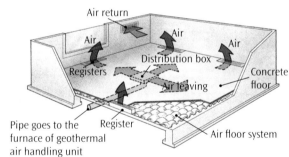

Air return

Air

Air

Air

Distribution box

Registers

Concrete floor

Air leaving

Pipe goes to the furnace of geothermal air handling unit

Register

Air floor system

Radiant cooling, radiant heating plus mechanical filtered ventilation

The Airfloor system uses air instead of water to heat and cool the house; most radiant systems only provide heat. A series of hollow, interlocking metal channels are placed on the subfloor and covered with concrete. When the system is activated, air is forced through the network of forms, creating a radiant floor and ventilating system. In the Smith house, the heated or cooled air from a geothermal heating system is pumped into the floor.

house, and rooms that serve multiple functions. "Because of the longevity of the house, we wanted to make sure that it could meet the needs of other families many years from now," Jackie says.

Passive and Active Systems

As much effort went into ways to conserve energy. The house was oriented to take best advantage of the sun. The taller south side collects more solar heat; the north side houses the garage and service area, which require less heat. Sun shades extending over the upper windows were angled so that in the summer when the sun is high, windows are shaded, while in the winter when the sun is low, sun floods the rooms and provides extra warmth.

The Smiths chose a geothermal heating system, which loops deep underground to tap the relatively constant temperature of the earth. In the winter, that constant temperature is carried back to the house to raise the temperature; in summer, it lowers the interior temperature.

The Airfloor was laid on top of prefabricated panels and covered with concrete.

A greenhouse was built against one side of the house so Jackie could grow a variety of plants.

Ordinarily, this process is straightforward and involves pumping air through a system of ducts to each room. In this house, however, the conditioned air is pumped into an innovative modular floor system called Airfloor (see the sidebar on the facing page). Because this house is in Illinois, supplemental electric heat kicks in when the temperature in the house drops more than two degrees below the desired temperature.

Oak trees that were removed from the property to build the house were milled into boards on site to conserve resources. Steve set up a shop in the garage basement and used the wood to build various trim, cabinets, and a mantel. He eventually plans to make furniture for the house from the remaining wood.

The Solarcrete construction also helps save on heating and cooling. The thermal mass of the concrete helps maintain a comfortable temperature all year. On summer evenings, the Smiths open windows to let in air that cools the house. In the morning, they close the windows and the concrete continues to radiate cool air. In the winter, when the heating

The concrete floor in the kitchen is stained three different colors to add a decorative effect. Stress joints were cut into the floor to add to the design but also to encourage any cracking to appear at those joints. Unfortunately, the concrete did not cooperate and cracked in another location.

system is on, the Solarcrete walls absorb heat and at night slowly radiate it to provide a good sleeping temperature.

A Comfortable Concrete Home

It took the contractor about four months to erect the Solarcrete panel exterior. A layer of stucco was applied to the exterior walls; drywall was hung on most interior walls.

The design was meant to take advantage of its stunning site and to be a venue for entertainment on a big scale. Farr designed this home with a sense of the outdoors—nearly every room has an outdoor view in two or more directions. Another design requirement was the ability to seat a large dinner gathering. To accommodate up to 30 people around a long stretch of tables, doors on overhead tracks slide out of the way, expanding the dining room into the parlor.

Farr says this house is perfectly suited for airline pilots, which both Jackie and Steve are. Their ability to keep all of the systems straight, takes a person used to flying a 727 with all of the systems—rudders, flaps and navigation. He says, "This house has some aspects of a plane in complexity."

The Smiths can enjoy cool outdoor breezes bug free in their screened-in porch.

Jesse Road House

Architect
JAWA Studio

Manufacturer
Precast
Technologies
of Nevada

Builder
John Simmons

Location
Henderson, NV

Square Footage
4,300 sq. ft.

Photography
© Ken Gutmaker,
except where noted

PREFABRICATED CONCRETE HOUSES PROBABLY aren't for everyone. But the Nevada attorney who owns this house will never go back to an ordinary framed house. His concrete-panel house is quieter, more solid, and is a better insulator against Nevada's famously hot summers.

Although insulated concrete panels have been used commercially for nearly 30 years, the system is new to the home market. Only about 50 houses across the United States have been built with insulated concrete panels. But panel makers, hoping to build more, have simplified the connection between panels and foundation and made them less visible than those used in commercial buildings. They also can cast wood nailers into the panels so that trim can be easily attached to hide the metal connectors that hold the panels to the foundation.

Of course, planning is critical with unforgiving concrete. For instance, extra conduits and outlet boxes are installed in the panels to prepare for future needs. It is key in this type of construction to know the location of every outlet so expensive cuts to add or relocate outlets won't be needed.

The exterior is reminiscent of traditional Spanish houses with exposed rafters and a concrete tiled roof (above). The garage section of the house is being set with a crane (left). Photo at left courtesy The Dow Chemical Company

Concrete Roof Tiles

Originally designed in Europe, concrete roof tiles have grown in popularity because of their resistance to fire, hail, wind, and heat. Concrete roof tiles are usually warranted for the life of the house. They are costlier than asphalt shingles but less expensive than clay tiles. Although concrete tiles are typically considered Mediterranean, they come in other colors than the traditional Mediterranean red and are made in a variety of shapes and sizes, even simulating the appearance of wood shakes, slate, and stone.

The barn was built to house the owner's horse during the winter months.

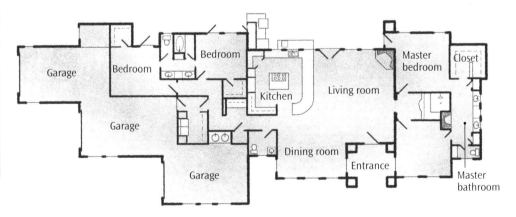

The louvers on the plantation shutters can be adjusted to admit light when desired.

A tubular fence was erected close to the house so the owners can look out the rear windows and watch their horse.

The 42 insulated concrete panels for this house were erected in a single day with the aid of a crane. If there hadn't been a delay in the delivery of the roof trusses, the house would have been completed in about four months instead of the six it took. Another problem was the existence on the site of a great deal of caliche, a rock found in the Southwest. It is costly to excavate, which makes it nearly prohibitive to dig basements. So like most houses in the area, this one was built on a concrete slab.

Much of the design of the house was in keeping with Southwest heritage. The house has concrete roof tiles, which are a practical alternative to clay tiles but have the same traditional look. The exposed rafter tails, or vigas, are also reminiscent of Spanish-style houses. Inside, plantation shutters were installed to keep out the hot desert sun. The shutters, while largely functional, give a finished look to the rooms.

The large sitting area by the island in the kitchen serves as a convenient location for guests to sit and chat with the cook.

Steel

p 196 Toronto, Canada | 3,400 sq. ft.

Steel frames were once used only in commercial construction, but North American companies have begun providing prefabricated steel frames for residential use—to good results. Metal systems include light-gauge, which is typically a replacement for wood stud framing, and heavy-gauge red iron (coated with a red oxide that resists rust), which is used as post-and-beam construction. Innovative techniques are also being developed by firms such as FACE Design (see pp. 208–215), where the steel frame and SIPs support the house.

Dunkirk, MD | 7,200 sq. ft.   p 202

Branford, CT | 5,300 sq. ft.   p 208

Homes built with steel framing are less vulnerable to fire, mold, rot, and insect damage. The manufacturer cuts and fits the frame, producing less waste and higher-quality fabrication and assembly under controlled conditions. Steel is also one of the most recyclable materials used in construction.

And where wood can twist, bow, warp, crack, split, and check, steel stays straight and strong. Steel can span longer distances than wood and withstand hurricanes and earthquakes if properly used.

Speed and Agility

The system designed by FACE Design (see p. 208) has the advantage of fewer parts than most steel-framed homes, which makes construction much faster. Coupled with SIPs, a steel-framed house requires few interior structural walls or columns, providing larger interior spaces and more design flexibility. The system also makes remodeling easier because interior walls can be easily reconfigured.

Many manufacturers use computers to evaluate the structural requirements of a house, taking into consideration interior walls, siding, roofing, and potential site conditions such as high wind and earthquakes. They are also built to code standards.

Excalibur Steel Structures, which built the House on Patuxent River (see p. 202), uses this computer system. The company evaluates requirements and designs the framing accordingly. The components are then cut in the factory and shipped to the site to be erected.

The plan for the Lumley House (see p. 196) was generated with the use of a computer, which figured engineering calculations based on the house size, weight, and site conditions.

Panels or sections for framing the floor, siding, and roofing are constructed with light-gauge steel in much the same way that a typical floor would be.

The frame for the Branford Point House was engineered in the architect's factory, where a unique tubular frame was preconstructed with a barnlike shape. Photo courtesy FACE Design

A light-gauge metal frame was used for the Lumley House in Toronto because of its strength and efficiency of construction. Photo courtesy KML Building Solutions

A red iron frame was used for the House on Patuxent River so it could support the first floor that spanned across two basements divided by a ravine that ran through the property. Photo courtesy Thomas K. Reinecker, Architect

Sections are labeled for easy installation and come with openings for windows and doors. Panels can measure up to 12 ft. by 26 ft. and in some cases can be installed in a day.

Its Time Has Come

One reason steel isn't used more often in home building is the difficulty in finding contractors experienced with using it. Generally, steel contractors are accustomed to building only commercial structures. But with the dwindling supply of good framing wood and increased demand for steel structures, more contractors will frame with steel and more manufacturers will produce custom steel framing for houses.

Lumley House

Manufacturer
KML Building
Solutions

Architect
Renée Durham
Pestrin, Caryatid
Architecture &
Design Inc.

AJ Tregebov
Architect

Builder
Meldazy
Construction

Location
Bennington,
Toronto, Canada

Square Footage
3,400 sq. ft.

Photography
Paul Eckhoff

RENÉE AND GLEN PESTRIN WANTED THEIR new house to have a streamlined, clean, contemporary design. Ordinarily, two people who share a common taste in architecture would gather a collection of home-design books and pages torn from magazines to explain to an architect what they wanted. In some cases, the architect would get it right away; in other cases, he or she might be unable to translate those ideas into workable plans.

However, the Pestrins had that problem solved. Renée, an architect, came up with the design ideas, and Glen, who is experienced in construction, knew how to turn Renée's plans into reality.

Glen, who likes the look of commercial and industrial building materials, wanted to build the house around a steel frame. Steel is a more predictably reliable than wood because it doesn't rot, insects can't harm it, and water and fire are not prime concerns. So the stability of steel and the time savings realized during the construction process were additional incentives for the couple to choose a prefabricated steel frame.

The front wall of the house has a water feature with water cascading over the top of the wall into a pool in the inner courtyard. Renée says the sound of the water acts as a wonderful sound buffer from the urban noise close by (above). A diverse grouping of natural materials can be seen on the exterior of the house including natural stone, stucco, copper, and the cherry stained wood that surrounds all of the glass (left).

Library/sitting room

Children's bedroom

Bedroom

Master bedroom

Bath

Bedroom

Master bath

Second Floor

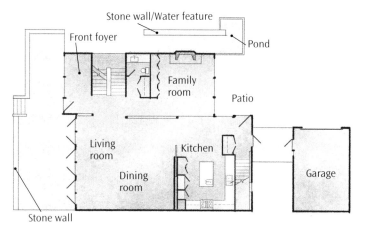

Stone wall/Water feature

Front foyer

Pond

Family room

Patio

Living room

Kitchen

Dining room

Garage

Stone wall

First Floor

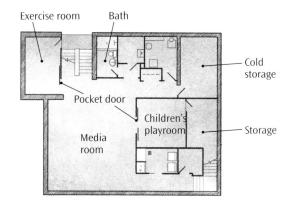

Exercise room

Bath

Cold storage

Pocket door

Children's playroom

Storage

Media room

Lower Level

The Pestrins purchased a steel-frame package that was zinc coated for corrosion resistance. But rather than having a truckful of steel studs show up on site, they hired Canadian KML Building Solutions to prefabricate the frame in panels and to erect it on site.

All walls were prefabricated in KML's facility with panels much like those in a wood system. KML also supplied the insulation, sheathing, red steel beams and columns where needed, panelized steel roof sections, and a composite floor system.

KML erected the shell of the house on top of a poured insulated concrete form foundation system (see the sidebar on p. 205). The builder, Meldazy Construction, installed the plumbing and electrical systems and windows and doors, applied the interior and exterior finishes, and completed the construction.

Three sets of French doors lead from the living room to the front courtyard.

A House of Stone, Steel, and Glass

The house is a model of clean lines and angles, visible in the geometry of the exterior, in the flush trim throughout, and in the abundance of pocket doors (see the sidebar on p. 201) that slide into the wall. Renée even designed the drainage system in a way that eliminated the need for gutters and downspouts because they would detract from the lines of the house. This type of system requires a flat roof that slants toward a center drain that carries rain and melted snow to the basement, where it is pumped out.

The strength of the metal frame made it possible to use an abundance of glass, which Renée needed to open up the house to its exterior surroundings. Doors leading out to the deck or to one of the patios allow the physical access; large spans of glass in transoms and doubled-up windows provide the visual access to the outdoors.

In the front foyer is one of the many paintings in the house by Erica Shuttleworth, who is a friend of the Pestrins.

Commercial-grade appliances and the stainless-steel backsplash reflect the light, creating a nice contrast with the dark walnut cabinets.

The sitting room on the second floor is a great place for Renee to read with her children before bed. During the day, the double windows flood this area with light, creating an excellent place for adults to read and relax.

Glen, who runs a marble, tile, and terrazzo business, used these materials in unique ways throughout the house. Stone is used on bathroom floors and on several walls, including one in the living room and foyer. In the kitchen and bathrooms, countertops are stone. Even the large pocket door in the living area is made of translucent onyx, which allows light to pass through.

The Pestrins enjoyed mixing natural materials. Stone faces the lower exterior walls and patio surfaces. The second-story walls are stuccoed. The windows are framed in pine, and water features are prominent both in the front and the rear of the house. Renée says the sound of water dulls the urban noise. Inside, the floors that aren't stone are black walnut.

The wall in the family room is limestone and the cabinetry is black walnut. Renée designed this unit to hide a multitude of wires and ducts that run from the basement to the second floor.

Pocket Doors

Around since the mid-19th century, pocket doors are a good way to open a room without wasting space. Pocket doors hang from a track and slide in and out of an open area framed inside the wall. They take up less room than doors that swing out—which require about 10 sq. ft. of floor area—and provide larger openings than traditional doors. Pocket doors were popular in Victorian-style houses at the turn of the 19th century, but the doors had tracks across the floor and presented a tripping hazard.

Today, top-hung doors are the norm because they move more smoothly and are less likely to stick. Kits come with hardware and materials to simplify installation and improve upon the movement of existing pocket doors.

The small sitting area to the side of the kitchen is a perfect place to sit and read while food is simmering on the stove or baking in the oven.

House on Patuxent River

PROBLEMS WITH A BUILDING SITE—WHETHER it's hilly, soggy, rocky, contains too much clay, or is too close to water— directly bear on the type of house that gets built. Here, where a ravine runs through the middle of the site, these challenges combined to form an opportunity.

To make the site work, Victor and Julie Cornellier were forced to build a house with two basements, one on each side of a ravine, connected by the first floor. For solid support, they decided to build a prefabricated heavy-gauge iron frame.

Victor had been in the construction business for years as a commercial glass contractor/manufacturer and served as his own general contractor, figuring he would "avoid most of the traps and pitfalls that others experience in building a house." Friend and architect Tom Reinecker designed the house.

Architect
Thomas K. Reinecker, Architect

Manufacturer
Excalibur Steel Structures

Steel Contractor
Steel Castle Structural

Location
Dunkirk, MD

Square Footage
7,200 sq. ft.

Photography
Phillip Jensen-Carter, except where noted

The Building Process

Excalibur Steel Structures converted Reinecker's architectural design into drawings, building to code requirements for wind resistance and window and door location. The frame was fabricated

The house was placed close to the river to take advantage of the beautiful views (above). The steel frame was all precut in a factory and transported to the site to be erected. Red steel was chosen because of its ability to span the two separate foundations and support the structure (left). Photo at left courtesy Thomas K. Reinecker

The large patio is a favorite gathering place in the warmer months. Architect Reinecker designed an open railing so people can see the water while sitting at the outdoor table.

The stone archways over the ravine allow for access to the front and rear portions of the basement.

in Excalibur's Chattanooga, Tennessee, plant, numbered and color-coded, and shipped to the site.

The iron frame included all of the structural "red" iron components (coated with red oxide to resist rust) for the three floors, lighter gauge studs and fasteners, and plans for erecting the structure. Parts were welded where needed and holes punched for fasteners. Framing went quickly—six months to engineer the frame (during which time the foundation was constructed) and three weeks to erect it. The house has since weathered two tornados with no structural damage.

After the frame went up, the house came together much like a wood-framed structure. Plywood sheathing was attached, followed by a vapor barrier, and fiber cement siding for durability and its long warranty. The lower exterior walls were faced with Carderock® stone from a quarry in Northern Virginia. The stone comes in blues, browns, grays, and greens; the Cornelliers used all of the colors and varied them throughout.

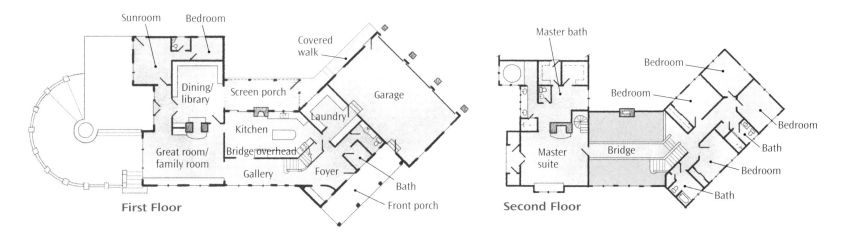

Sunroom Bedroom

Covered walk

Dining/ library

Screen porch

Garage

Kitchen

Laundry

Great room/ family room

Bridge overhead

Gallery

Foyer

Bath

Front porch

First Floor

Master bath

Bedroom

Bedroom

Bedroom

Master suite

Bridge

Bath

Bedroom

Bath

Second Floor

Insulated Concrete Form Foundations

When a foundation is poured, fresh concrete flows into plywood forms. Once the concrete cures, the forms are removed. Unlike standard forms, insulated concrete forms (ICFs) remain to provide insulation. When the ICF sections are installed, windows and doors are cut out, rebar is installed, and concrete poured to create an insulated structural wall. A stack of six such forms builds an 8-ft.-high basement. ICF systems are installed faster than poured concrete foundations and create walls with high energy efficiency, sound resistance, and strength. Their cost is about the same as traditional foundations.

The triangular window in the second-story office is strategically placed to take full advantage of the river view.

All of the moldings in the house are finished with a fluted edge; they are lovely with the Brazilian Santos mahogany floor shown here.

The flooring—a stable, dark reddish-brown wood—was cut from a sustainable forest. The natural light pouring in from the generous skylights adds warmth to this walkway.

Designed for the Long Haul

Victor chose steel because of its strength and durability. He and Julie expect their home will outlive them and will provide shelter for future generations. They also chose a prefabricated insulated concrete form foundation (see the sidebar on p. 205) over a typical foundation because of its energy efficiency. The roof is standing-seam copper, which is durable, lasts a lifetime, and oxidizes to a lovely patina. And the overlapping sheets of copper make a strong, watertight roof.

Large commercial light fixtures span the kitchen, supplementing the recessed lighting along the sides and those high up in the angled ceiling.

Because of the Cornelliers' appreciation of the local habitat, they commissioned an artist to paint a large mural that covers an entire wall and includes many of the native birds that can be seen by the river, including the eagles that nest there.

Design of the frame is similar to post–and–beam construction, with the outer frame providing the structural support. Victor wanted the entire house to be extremely rigid so he framed interior walls with light–gauge steel. Because the iron post–and–beam frame bears the weight of the roof and floors, the interior walls were not required to be structural, which allows for open interior spaces and simplified remodeling.

Exterior and Interior Details

A distinctive characteristic of this house is its outrigger, or overhang, which Reinecker designed for each window on the south side of the house. These serve as awnings to protect the windows and block summer sunlight from heating the interior.

The rear of the house facing the river was designed in a contemporary style, while the front was designed with porch and dormers. A walkway connecting the two sections on the second floor sits under a vaulted ceiling, each side featuring three 6-ft. square skylights that flood the house with light.

Branford Point House

Architect
FACE Design: Sean Tracy, Todd Fouser, Reuben Jorsling

Manufacturer
FACE Design

Builder
Gary Frohlich Builders

Location
Branford, CT

Square Footage
5,300 sq. ft.

Photography
Phillip Jensen-Carter

BUILDING THEIR MASSIVE INDUSTRIAL-STYLE retirement home was a family affair for Peter and Jane Tracy. They hired their son Sean, an architect, to design a prefabricated house with plenty of open space that took the best advantage of natural light, views, and breezes coming off Long Island Sound.

The Tracys' first challenge was finding the right lot, which proved fairly simple. They discovered a narrow, 1.2-acre lot on the banks of the Branford River that had the water views they wanted. On the property was an old boarding house and, behind it, a smaller house, where the owner lived. The Tracys made an offer for both and the owner accepted.

The Tracys asked Sean for a comfortable home that worked with its waterfront location, required minimal maintenance, and could be prefabricated. The house also should have large, open spaces with few interior walls that would limit floor-plan options. Because this was to be their retirement house, they also wanted plenty of work-space. Peter needed space to work on his music and documentary films; Jane

The site for the house was selected for its proximity to the water so Peter could go sailing and fishing. The placement of the windows and porches was designed to take advantage of the beautiful water views (above). The house is seen from across the river in Branford Point (left).

The upper level of the house is divided into two sections that are connected with an outside open roof deck, which the Tracys use for relaxing and watching the river views.

needed a large art studio. The Tracys also required large windows for views of the river and for fresh air.

Sean and partners Todd Fouser and Reuben Jorsling founded FACE Design, which specializes in innovative interior spaces for commercial structures. The Tracy home would be FACE Design's first residential project, but it was a good match. Sean and his partners stay involved throughout construction and prefer to produce many of the architectural elements they design for a space (such as stairs, windows, doors, lighting fixtures, and furniture) in their Brooklyn shop.

Armed with their list, Sean and his partners set out to give his parents just what they wanted. They decided that the best layout for the narrow lot would be two structures connected by a breezeway downstairs and an open roof deck upstairs. Breaking up the house in this way helps visu–

ally "reduce" the size of the house. The breezeway and upper deck let them take advantage of mild weather. Inside, the larger of the two structures includes the common areas, Jane's studio, and the master suite. The guest suite, spa area with wave pool, garage, and Peter's studio are in the smaller structure.

Unique Construction and Materials

To increase efficiency and save construction time, Sean and his partners prefabricated as much of the house as possible. The main structure of the house is a series of 13 metal-tube arches that were prefabricated in the FACE Design factory and lifted into place by crane. To make the house tight and comfortable during the cold Connecticut winters, SIPs, sandwiches of high-density foam between panels of oriented-strand board, were installed between the steel arches. The company that made the panels, Panel Pros of New Hampshire, rounded the rectangular panels to fit the curved frame of the house.

A beautiful aspect of the house is the structural arches and supports that can be seen throughout the house.

Although the Tracys' house is more modern than neighboring houses, it fits in beautifully with its environment. The surfaces are softened by the abundance of surrounding foliage.

FACE designed and built the front entrance door, which is made of steel and glass.

In addition to the steel arches, or girders, much of the rest of the house was also made in FACE Design's Brooklyn factory. Because they're from a single source of design and fabrication, custom structural items such as the tempered-glass and steel staircase, railings, interior sliding glass doors that separate the pantry and office from the great room, frosted glass partitions in the upstairs bedrooms, and the metal-glass-wood front door give the house a design unity not often possible.

For the siding, staircase, and interior railings, they chose a South American hardwood called ipe (pronounced EE-pay), or ironwood, which is extremely dense and durable. Unlike other exotic hardwoods, such as mahogany, ipe is a fast-growing, sustainable wood.

A unique wall assembly that supports the kitchen cabinets and shelves provides storage while maintaining water views from the kitchen. The overhead lighting in the dining room was a team effort between Sean and his mother. Jane hired a glassblower to fabricate glass tubes that FACE Design turned into light fixtures in their factory. The glass lights hang from a prefabricated interior beam that spans the room.

The architects call this a "rural industrial archetype," consistent with the barn form they are attracted to.

The limited need for interior partitions gives the Tracys' house an open and airy feeling.

The roof is Galvalum®, a steel sheet that's finished with a colored aluminum zinc alloy for corrosion resistance. The metal roof was also formed to specification in the factory. Another custom creation, the metal garage door with windows was finished to match the color of the roof.

New Challenges Met

FACE Design developed several structural innovations to make this project work. A special "clip" was fabricated to attach the SIP panels to the girders. A concern that the metal arches might transmit cold to the inside of the house led the architects to add high-density insulation over the metal on the exterior.

Just as the SIPs needed to be curved to work between the rounded girders, the drywall also needed to be curved. The architects and builder determined that two layers of ⅜-in. drywall would bend to the shape and add up to match the ¾-in. drywall on the flat part of the walls and ceiling.

Raising the structural metal frame took a week; finessing the SIP panels into perfect placement took another month. Once the structure was up, builders took 11 months to complete the interior and exterior construction.

First Floor

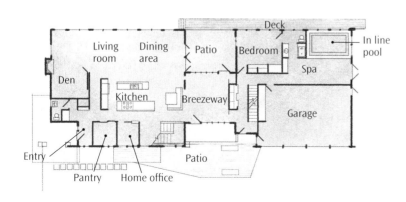

Second Floor

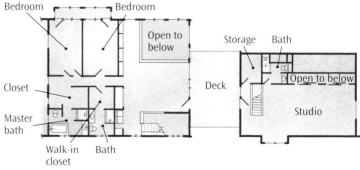

The staircase, which was prefabricated in the FACE Design factory, is made of steel with ipe wood treads and tempered-glass sides.

Garage doors were custom-made in a commercial factory so they would match the steel used for the structure.

Financial Arrangements with Contractors

Because of the uniqueness of the FACE Design plan, the Tracys knew it would be difficult for builders to adequately bid the project. Peter approached Gary Frohlich, a builder he'd worked with before. Peter offered Frohlich an hourly rate, plus the cost of materials, rather than the typical fixed-fee arrangement.

Typical Arrangements Between Homeowners and General Contractors

■ **Fixed-fee contract** After evaluating the cost of materials and labor, a general contractor gives the homeowner a total cost for building the house, which is agreed upon in a contract. Changes in design or materials after the contract is signed cost extra.

■ **Modified fixed-fee contract** This is similar to the fixed-fee arrangement except that certain items, such as bathroom fixtures and audio systems, are left out of the contract and are the responsibility of the homeowner.

■ **Cost-plus contract** The general contractor gives the homeowner a price for the supervision of subcontractors, coordination of the project, and purchasing all materials. The homeowner is responsible for all labor and material costs. Sometimes the general contractor will receive a percentage of the cost of the labor and materials as additional compensation.

Resources

Modular

Moose Creek Lodge
Manufacturer
American Timbercraft
2382 N. 1500 W.
Farr West, UT 84404
801-782-7820
www.americantimbercraft.com

Chez Poupon
Architect
Mike Gentile, P.C.
761 Walnut Ave.,
Bohemia, NY 11716
631-218-3853

Manufacturer
Haven Homes, Inc.
554 Eagle Valley Rd.
Beech Creek, PA 16822
570-962-2111
www.havenhomes.com

Builder
Barry Altman
The Builder, Inc.
Box 916
Quogue, NY 11959
800-843-2537
631-288-1749

Sunset Breezehouse
Architect
Michelle Kaufmann
Designs + Sunset
www.mkd-arc.com
info@mkd-arc.com

Manufacturer
Britco Structures, Ltd.
V4N 4G1
Surrey, BC, Canada V4N 4G1
800-527-4826
www.britco.com

Builder
De Mattei Construction, Inc.
1794 The Alameda
San Jose, CA 95126
408-350-4200
www.demattei.com

Maryfield House
Architect
Hall & Hull Architects, Inc.
P.O. Box 5216
Hilton Head Island, SC 29938
843-815-2929
www.hallandhull.com

Manufacturer
Nationwide Homes, Inc.
1100 Rives Rd., P.O. Box 5511
Martinsville, VA 24115
800-216-7001

Builder
Jack Harris
Daufuskie Holdings, Inc.,
5 Fen Ct.
Savannah, GA 31411-1336

Supplier
Hardiplank
www.jameshardie.com

Panelized

Coastal House
Architect
Doug Govan, AIA
Empyrean International, LLC
930 Main St.
Acton, MA 01720
800-727-3325
www.deckhouse.com

Manufacturer
Empyrean International, LLC
930 Main St.
Acton, MA 01720
800-727-3325
www.deckhouse.com

Builder
Lauer Construction
1912a Lincoln Dr.
Annapolis, MD 21410
800-841-6203

Interior Design
Polly Dithmer

Lighting Specialist
Susan Arnold
Wolfers Lighting

Suppliers
Energy Star program
www.energystar.gov

LTI Smart Glass
www.ltismartglass.com

Pella® Windows
www.pella.com

Teragren™ LLC (Bamboo)
www.teragren.com

WeatherBest® Decking
www.lpcorp.com

Cultured Stone® by
Owens Corning®
www.culturedstone.com

Hardiplank
www.jameshardie.com

Greenridge House
Architect
McCormack +
Etten/Architects
400 Broad St.
Lake Geneva, WI 53147
262-248-8391
www.mccormacketten.com

Manufacturer
Sterling Building Systems/
Wausau Homes
P.O. Box 8005
Wausau, WI 54402-8005
715-359-7272
www.SterlingBldg.com

Builder
Engerman Contracting
Lake Geneva, WI
262-248-9210
www.engermancontracting.com

Interior Design
Diane Albrecht,
Paper Dolls Home Furnishing

Supplier
Vetter Windows
www.vetterwindows.com

Pfaff House
Architect
David Marlatt, AIA
DNM Architect
161 Natoma St.
San Francisco, CA 94105
415-348-8910
www.dnm-architect.com

Manufacturer
Nelson Homes
5027 44th St.
Lloydminster, SK, Canada
P9V 0A6
800-661-6534
www.nelson-homes.com

Suppliers
CWD Windows and Doors
www.cwdwindows.com

Wicanders® Cork Flooring
Amorim Flooring North
America
www.wicanders.com

Myson® (radiators)
www.mysoninc.com

Hardiplank
www.jameshardie.com

SIPs

Villa Kaki
Architect
John D. Jarrard
John D. Jarrad Architect–
Planner
1700 S. Spring St.
Little Rock, AR 72206
501-375-4249

Manufacturer
Fischer SIPS
1843 Northwestern Pkwy.
Louisville, KY 40203
800-792-7477
www.fishersips.com

Builder
Hydco, Inc.
208 N. Beech St.
North Little Rock, AR 72114
501-371-0255
www.hydco.com

Interior Design
Kaki Hockersmith
Kaki Hockersmith Interiors
1408 Rebsamen Park Rd.
Little Rock, AR 72202
501-666-6966
www.kakihockersmith.com

Supplier
Chadsworth 1-800 Columns
www.columns.com

Chaleff House
Architect
Bill Chaleff, RA
Chaleff and Rogers, Architects
P.O. Box 990
Water Mill, NY 11976
631-726-4477

Builder
Germano Contracting
631-329-1882

Supplier
Hardiplank
www.jameshardie.com

Timber Frame

Craftsman's Lodge
Designer
Steve Petty
Davis Frame Co., Inc.
P.O. Box 1079
Claremont, NH 03743
800-636-0993
www.davisframe.com

Manufacturer
Davis Frame Co., Inc.
P.O. Box 1079
Claremont, NH 03743
800-636-0993
www.davisframe.com

Builder
Miller Starbuck Construction
P.O. Box 726
Falmouth, MA 02541
508-539-1124
http://millerstarbuck.com/
thebasics.html

Suppliers
Hearth & Home Technologies™
www.heatilator.com

Cabot
www.cabotstain.com

Interior Design
Corinha Designs
26 York Rd.
Mansfield, MA 02048

The Queenslander
Architect
Howard Holtzman
Howard Holtzman and
Associates
Kildeer, IL
847-438-7225

Manufacturer
Riverbend Timber Framing
P.O. Box 26
Blissfield, MI 49228
517-486-4355
www.riverbendtf.com

Builder
Carlson Construction
Michigan City, IN
219-879-5186
www.carlson-construction.com

Supplier
Halquist Stone
www.halquiststone.com

House on the Saltwater Marsh
Architect
Hal Minick
J.A. Minick International
Hendersonville, NC
828-272-9113

Manufacturer
Tommi Jamison
Hearthstone, Inc.
1630 E. Highway 25/70
Dandridge, TN 37725
800-247-4442
www.hearthstonehomes.com

Suppliers
Hardiplank
www.jameshardie.com

Gerard Roofing Technologies
www.gerardusa.com

GeoDeck™
www.geodeck.com

Bainbridge Island House
Manufacturer
Timbercraft Homes
85 Martin Rd.
Port Townsend, WA 98368
360-385-3051
www.timbercraft.com

Builder
Bluefish Fine Builders
7755 Westerly Ln., NE
Bainbridge Island, WA 98110
206-842-4544

Supplier
Kolbe Windows & Doors
www.kolbe-kolbe.com

Hobbit Haven
Architect
Edwin Ugorowski
Bitterroot Design Group
37 E. Main St., Ste. #7
Bozeman, MT 59715
406-587-2390
www.bitterrootgroup.com

Manufacturer
Bitterroot Timberframes
659 Spruce Drive
Big Sky, MT 59716
406-995-7806

Supplier
Durfeld Log & Timber
Williams Lake, BC, Canada
250-989-0555
www.durfeldlogandtimber.com

Far Horizon Reflection Home
Architect
James Cutler
Cutler Anderson Architects
135 Parfitt Way SW
Bainbridge Island, WA 98110
206-842-4710
www.cutler-anderson.com

Manufacturer
Lindal Cedar Homes
4300 South 104th Place
Seattle, WA 98178
206-892-1254
www.lindal.com

Builder
Innsbrook Custom Homes
1 Aspen Circle
Innsbrook, MO 63390
636-745-3000, ext. 225

Supplier
Reveal Designs
www.reveal-designs.com

Interior Design
Frank Patton Interiors, Inc.
13133 Manchester Rd.
St. Louis, MO 63131
314-965-4240

Log Construction

Idaho Chalet
Architect
g.d. Longwell Architects
The Fairways Professional Center
E. 1677 Miles Ave., Ste. 100
Hayden Lake, ID 83835
208-772-0503
www.gdlarch.com

Manufacturer
Caribou Creek Log Homes
HCR85, Box 3
Bonners Ferry, ID 83805
800-619-1156
www.caribou-creek.com

Builder
Campbell & Campbell, LLC
1110 E. Cherrywood Dr.
Couer D'Alene, ID 83814
208-660-5416

Crooked Pine Ranch
Architect
Gordon Hughes
Maple Island Log Homes
2387 Bayne Rd.
Twin Lake, MI 49457-9737
231-821-2151
www.mapleisland.com

Manufacturer
Maple Island Log Homes
2387 Bayne Rd.
Twin Lake, MI 49457-9737
231-821-2151
www.mapleisland.com

Builder
Steven Fox
Custom Log Structures

Interior Design
Lisa Simone
Simone Deary Group
605 North Michigan Ave.
Chicago, IL 60611
312-274-0606

Supplier
Country Furniture by Schulers
533 North Main St.
Jamesville, WI 53545
608-754-4052

Triple Run

Architect
Locati Architects
1007 E. Main St., Ste. 20
Bozeman, MT
406-587-1139
www.locatiarchitects.com

Builder
Bitterroot Timberframes
659 Spruce Dr.
Big Sky, MT 59716
406-995-7806
www.bitterrootgroup.com

Interior Design
Michelle Varda
Varda Interiors

Supplier
EcoStar Roofing Materials
www.premiumroofs.com

Country Dream House

Manufacturer
Barna Log Homes
22459 Alberta St.
Oneida, TN 37841
800-962-4734
www.barnahomes.com

Builder
Country Living Log Homes
3187 W.O.W. Rd.
Randleman, NC 27317
336-498-2893

Supplier
Superior Walls
www.superiorwalls.com

Gallatin River House

Architect
Edwin Ugorowski
Bitterroot Design Group
37 E. Main St., Ste. #7
Bozeman, MT 59715
406-587-2390
www.bitterrootgroup.com

Builder
Bitterroot Group
659 Spruce Dr.
Big Sky, MT 59716
406-995-7806
www.bitterrootgroup.com

Concrete

Smith House

Architect
Farr Associates
53 W. Jackson Blvd., Ste. 650
Chicago, IL 60604
312-408-1661
www.farrside.com

Manufacturer
National Solarcrete Inc.
230 N. Maple St.
Payne, OH 45880
419-263-1333
www.solarcrete.com

Suppliers
Airfloor
Aero Systems
212 S. Milwaukee Ave.
Wheeling, IL 60090
847-459-6080
www.airfloor.com

H Window
401 17th Ave. W.
Ashland, WI 54806
800-843-4929
www.hwindow.com

Jesse Road House

Architect
David Ellerton
JAWA Studio
103 E. Charleston Blvd.
Las Vegas, NV 89104
702-598-1723

Manufacturer
Precast Technology
6020 N. Hollywood Blvd.
Las Vegas, NV 89115
702-991-0400

Supplier
The Dow Chemical Company
200 Larkin Center, 1605 Joseph
Dr., Midland, MI 48674
866-583-BLUE
www.styrofoam.com/architect

Builder
John Simmons

Steel

Lumley House

Architect
Renee Pestrin Architect & AJ
Tregebov Architect
16 Birch Ave., Ste. 101
Toronto, ON, Canada M4V 1C8
416-823-7681

Manufacturer
KML Building Solutions
1139 Industrial Rd.
Cambridge, ON, Canada
N3H 4W3
519-653-2159
www.kmlbuildingsolutions.com

Builder
Meldazy Construction
173 Homewood Ave.
Willowdale, Toronto, ON,
Canada M2M 1K4
416-223-8433

Suppliers
Cambria® (Engineered Stone)
www.cambriausa.com

Ridley Windows & Doors
www.ridley-windows.com

Erica Shuttleworth (Artist)
www.ericashuttleworth.com

House on Patuxent River

Architect
Thomas K. Reinecker
12002 Palisades Dr.
Dunkirk, MD 20754
301-855-9020

Manufacturer
Excalibur Steel Structures
8-A Francis St.
Chattanooga, TN 37419
423-825-0022
www.excalibursteel.com

Steel Contractor
Vince Oliver
Steel Castle Structural
201 Archer Hill Rd.
Follansbee, WV 26037
304-527-5100
voliver@weir.net

Suppliers
Arxx Building Products
www.arxxwalls.com

Hardiplank
www.jameshardie.com

Gerard Roofing Technologies
(Stone-Coated Roofing)
www.gerardusa.com

Branford Point House

Architect
FACE Design: Sean Tracy, Todd
Fouser, Reuben Jorsling
195 North 14th St.
Brooklyn, NY 11211
718-486-828
www.facedesign.com

Manufacturer
FACE Design: Sean Tracy, Todd
Fouser, Reuben Jorsling
195 North 14th St.
Brooklyn, NY 11211
718-486-828
www.facedesign.com

Builder
Gary Frohlich Builders
359 Clapboard Hill Rd.
Guilford, CT 06347
203-453-5485